THE BEST WAY TO
BETTER
GOLF

THE BEST WAY TO
BETTER
GOLF
NUMBER 2

Jack Nicklaus

A FAWCETT GOLD MEDAL BOOK
Fawcett Publications, Inc., Greenwich, Conn.
Member of American Book Publishers Council, Inc.

CONTENTS

Chapter 3 STRATEGY AND TROUBLE SHOTS 45

Chapter 4 FIRST-AID ON THE COURSE 69

Chapter 5 POWER AND ACCURACY 81

Introduction

Golfers of average or better-than-average scoring ability can, with certain reservations, predict the outcome of most of their shots. They know their strengths and their weaknesses. They are ready to make the necessary and sometimes minuscule adjustments in their game that will shave strokes from their scorecard. The gap between an 85 and an 80 is a large one, scoring-wise, but it can be bridged by upgrading technique.

That's what I hope to help you achieve in this book. I'm a strong believer in preparedness when it comes to golf. I'm also a strong believer in keeping golf instruction as simple as possible, because golf itself is not a simple game. As I explained in Volume I, I feel that one of the best ways to absorb instruction is by simple action illustrations that show, as well as tell, how to execute specific shots. By seeing graphically how they are made, you form a picture of it in your own mind and, with application, you can transmit this to your game. You learn by emulating.

The type of drawing used in this book is designed to give you instant identification. You will find in it golf problems that you recognize as your own. I think you'll also find the clues to overcoming these problems. I've arranged the book by chapters in the most practical way I know, dealing with separate phases of the game in each section. Some of the tips may appear to be fundamental, but remember, golf is a game of building; one layer goes over the next. If your basic techniques are weakened, your whole game will collapse on top of it.

But this is a time to think in positive terms. Approach this book with the same bright feelings of optimism you have on a clear, sunny day as you tee up on the first hole. Swing with assurance, but with an eye turned inward on that mental picture of yourself, and you will reach the next plateau.

JACK NICKLAUS

CHAPTER 1

Return to the Basics

It is a sad but fundamental truth about golf that the more you learn about playing the game, the more is apt to go wrong with it. This is especially true after a long layoff from one season to the next. Frankly, after months of tournament pressure, I find that parts of my swing have changed and I'm glad for the respite. If I were to continue from year to year without a pause, I could possibly multiply my errors.

To dedicated players, though, the enforced winter hiatus is a nuisance; but to look at it from the brighter side, it does give you a chance to reevaluate your game. Let's assume, then, that you've picked up this book at the start of a new golf season. If you're like most golfers I run across, you probably haven't held a club in your hands all winter, so you shouldn't expect to be in mid-season form your first time out. Keep in mind the fact that even professional ballplayers go through spring training, slowly working their way back into shape.

The first thing I generally do at the start of a new season is to check each part of my swing individually—my grip, stance, head position and the direction in which my feet are pointing. Obviously, flaws could have developed over the long winter, and I make any necessary adjustments. You should do the same. After you've had a long look at your swing (why not take some practice swings in front of your mirror?), do something about it right away. It could be something you can correct by yourself, such as a hitch in your swing; but if it's something more critical than that, you ought to see your professional.

Now, before turning you loose on this section of tuneups, let me give you one more word of counsel. I feel that everyone should start a little new each year. Don't expect to hit the ball as you did before the layoff. Make your comeback a gradual one, making sure everything is correct first.

11

GIVE IT A LITTLE EXTRA

ONE OF GOLF'S TOUGHEST SHOTS, AS YOU MAY AGREE, IS THAT FIRST DRIVE FROM THE FIRST TEE. IT IS ALSO ONE OF THE MOST IMPORTANT, AS IT CAN ESTABLISH A TEMPO FOR THE ENTIRE ROUND...

...IT'S NATURAL TO BE TENSE HERE, ESPECIALLY BEFORE THE USUAL FIRST TEE GALLERY, BUT NEVER HURRY JUST TO SHORTEN THE AGONY. A GOOD DRIVE WILL HELP BUILD CONFIDENCE FOR THE SHOTS TO FOLLOW. SO CONCENTRATE EXTRA ON MAKING THAT FIRST ONE NO LESS THAN PERFECT!

BARRETT TAYLOR

START with STRAIGHT WRISTS

ADDRESS POSITION OF THE WRISTS PLAYS A LARGE PART IN DETERMINING THE OUTCOME OF A SHOT...

LATERAL BEND WITH THE LEFT HAND BOWED CREATES A TENDENCY TO LIFT THE CLUB ABRUPTLY ON THE BACK-SWING AND THUS CAUSE A *HOOKING* ACTION AT IMPACT.

IF YOUR LEFT WRIST BREAKS IN, YOU MAY FIND YOUR-SELF TAKING THE CLUB OUTSIDE AND SLICING.

FOR BEST OVERALL CONTROL, KEEP YOUR HANDS VOID OF ANY SIDE BEND.

BARRETT TAYLOR

TWO THOUGHTS for SWINGING

ONCE FAMILIAR WITH THE MECHANICS OF A CORRECT GOLF STROKE, STUDENTS BEGIN TO WONDER HOW ONE REMEMBERS THEM ALL WHILE SWINGING. TRUTH IS, ONE DOESN'T, NOT CONSCIOUSLY AT LEAST. FOR THE 2 OR 3 SECONDS IT TAKES TO COMPLETE A SWING ALLOWS LITTLE TIME TO THINK.

1 *I THINK OF 2 THINGS: TAKING THE CLUB STRAIGHT BACK AS SLOWLY AS POSSIBLE...*

2 *...AND KEEPING MY HEAD STILL*

EACH PART OF THE SWING MUST BE THOUGHT OUT SEPARATELY IN PRACTICE UNTIL IT CAN BE PERFORMED AUTOMATICALLY. THEN, IN ACTUAL PLAY, 2 THOUGHTS, THOUGH THIS MAY DIFFER WITH THE INDIVIDUAL, IS ABOUT ALL TIME PERMITS.

"BARRETT TAYLOR"

IRONING OUT THE KINKS

QUITE OFTEN YOU CAN ELIMINATE A SWING FLAW MERELY BY SLOWING DOWN TEMPO.

PERHAPS YOU'VE ACQUIRED THE HABIT OF "LAYING OFF THE BALL" — A TERM THAT REFERS TO BREAKING THE WRISTS TOO SOON ON TAKEAWAY. PERHAPS YOU'RE NOT EVEN AWARE OF THIS, BUT YOU KNOW SOMETHING IS WRONG WITH YOUR SWING...

BARRETT TAYLOR

CONCENTRATING ON SWINGING THE CLUB BACK SLOWLY WILL HELP RETAIN THE STRAIGHT-LINE RELATION OF THE LEFT ARM AND CLUB.

THE SLOWER YOU SWING, THE GREATER YOUR CHANCE OF CORRECTING THE FAULT — A CASE OF IRONING OUT YOUR SWING THROUGH *SHEER CONCENTRATION!*

CENTER-UP *at* ADDRESS

AT ADDRESS THE CLUBFACE SHOULD BE CENTERED SO AS TO BE DIRECTLY IN LINE WITH THE BALL.

THE HABIT OF ADDRESSING THE BALL NEAR THE TOE OR HEEL OF THE CLUBHEAD IS ADDING ERROR TO ERROR, REQUIRING THAT SOMETHING BE CHANGED DURING THE DOWNSWING IN ORDER TO MEET THE BALL SQUARELY.

BARRETT TAYLOR.

ALWAYS ADDRESS THE BALL WHERE YOU WANT TO STRIKE IT. IF YOU FAIL TO STRIKE THE BALL SQUARELY AFTER LINING UP CORRECTLY, SOMEWHERE IN YOUR SWING OR STANCE IS A FLAW TO BE FOUND AND CORRECTED.

RIGHT ARM on the BACKSWING

WHEN TENSION CREEPS INTO THE RIGHT ARM AT ADDRESS AND DURING THE BACKSWING, CONTROL AND TEMPO ARE LOST.

START WITH THE RIGHT ARM RELAXED AND SLIGHTLY BENT, THEN LET IT REMAIN PASSIVE AS THE LEFT ARM PERFORMS THE TAKEAWAY.

THE RIGHT HAND SERVES AS A GUIDE TO HELP CONTROL THE CLUBHEAD, BUT THE RIGHT ARM MERELY GOES ALONG FOR THE RIDE.

BARRETT TAYLOR#

LEFT SHOULDER CONTROL

ONE OF THE MOST COMMON FAULTS OF THE HIGH HANDICAPPER IS A FLAT, OR LEVEL, SHOULDER TURN; THE BACKSWING. ALSO BECOMES FLAT, AS THE LEFT ELBOW FLIES OUT AND THE CLUBFACE IS 'LAID OFF.'

CORRECT SHOULDER TURN IS CONTROLLED BY THE **LEFT** SHOULDER, WHICH STARTS **DOWN** IMMEDIATELY AS THE CLUB AND BODY MOVE IN UNISON.

THE LEFT SHOULDER CONTINUES TO COME DOWN AND UNDER, THE RIGHT SHOULDER COMES UP AND THE CLUB GOES STRAIGHT BACK FROM THE BALL.

BARRETT TAYLOR

18

FULL SWING AID TO RHYTHM

IF YOU POSSESS A SHORT STYLE OF SWINGING OR HAVE SUBCONSCIOUSLY ACQUIRED AN ABBREVIATED BACKSWING, YOU MAY FIND IT DIFFICULT TO MAINTAIN PROPER TIMING AND RHYTHM.

IN ANY CASE, YOU CAN RESTORE TEMPO BY LENGTHENING THE BACKSWING.

BARRETT TAYLOR

YOU'LL FIND THAT A FULL HIP AND SHOULDER TURN WILL GIVE YOU MORE TIME IN WHICH TO BLEND MOVEMENTS SMOOTHLY.

KEEP LEFT HEEL LIFT TO A MINIMUM

LEFT HEEL LIFT ON THE BACKSWING IS MERELY A RESULT OF BODY TURN AND SHOULD NEVER OCCUR AS AN INDEPENDENT ACTION.

FROM THE THREE OR FOUR IRON DOWN THROUGH THE SHORT IRONS, AS BODY TURN LESSENS, THE LEFT HEEL NEED NOT LIFT AT ALL.

ACTUALLY, LEFT HEEL IS NOT A VITAL PART OF THE BACK-SWING. IT WOULD EVEN BE IDEAL IF THE LEFT HEEL REMAINED GROUNDED ON ALL SHOTS, FOR THIS WOULD ERASE ANY TENDENCY TO RETURN THE FOOT TO A DIFFERENT POSITION AND CHANGE THE SWING PLANE, A TENDENCY OF MANY GOLFERS, MYSELF INCLUDED.

THE DRIVER AND LONG CLUB SWING WILL FORCE THE LEFT HEEL TO RISE. THE BEST THING YOU CAN DO IS TO TRY AND KEEP THE LIFTING TO A MINIMUM.

LEFT HEEL NOTES

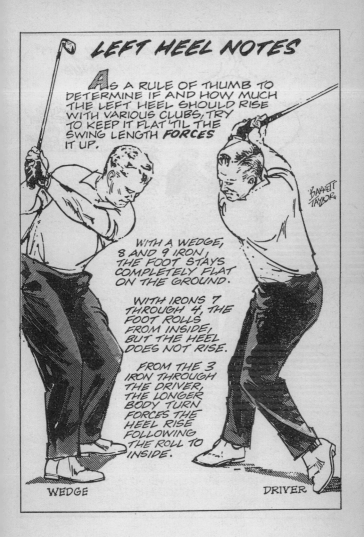

As a rule of thumb to determine if and how much the left heel should rise with various clubs, try to keep it flat 'til the swing length *FORCES* it up.

WITH A WEDGE, 8 AND 9 IRON, THE FOOT STAYS COMPLETELY FLAT ON THE GROUND.

WITH IRONS 7 THROUGH 4, THE FOOT ROLLS FROM INSIDE, BUT THE HEEL DOES NOT RISE.

FROM THE 3 IRON THROUGH THE DRIVER, THE LONGER BODY TURN FORCES THE HEEL RISE FOLLOWING THE ROLL TO INSIDE.

BARRETT TAYLOR

WEDGE

DRIVER

AVOID FLAT HIP-TURN

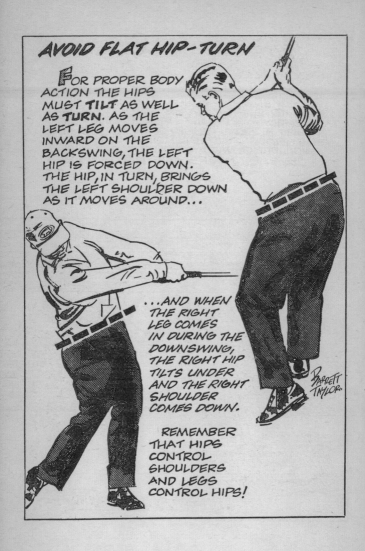

FOR PROPER BODY ACTION THE HIPS MUST **TILT** AS WELL AS **TURN**. AS THE LEFT LEG MOVES INWARD ON THE BACKSWING, THE LEFT HIP IS FORCED DOWN. THE HIP, IN TURN, BRINGS THE LEFT SHOULDER DOWN AS IT MOVES AROUND...

...AND WHEN THE RIGHT LEG COMES IN DURING THE DOWNSWING, THE RIGHT HIP TILTS UNDER AND THE RIGHT SHOULDER COMES DOWN.

REMEMBER THAT HIPS CONTROL SHOULDERS AND LEGS CONTROL HIPS!

BARRETT TAYLOR.

GETTING the RIGHT SIDE UNDER the SHOT

Delayed wrist action, the key to power, even accuracy, is largely a result of keeping the right elbow tucked in close to the body and bringing the right shoulder down and under as the clubhead enters the hitting area.

When the right elbow flies and the right shoulder rides high the result is the well known hit-from-the-top with a premature release and a forfeiture of impact speed and control.

BARRETT TAYLOR

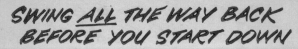

SWING <u>ALL</u> THE WAY BACK BEFORE YOU START DOWN

FOR A SMOOTH FLOW OF HANDS AND ARMS THRU THE HIT, BODY ACTION MUST BE PROPERLY TIMED.

A COMMON FAULT IS STARTING THE *DOWNSWING BEFORE THE BACKSWING IS FULLY COMPLETED.*

THE SUDDEN CHANGE IN BODY DIRECTION JERKS THE CLUB INTO A WHIPPY MOTION, CAUSING THE BLADE TO DESCEND TOO ABRUPTLY AND PRODUCE SOME PRETTY DEEP DIVOTS. SO GIVE YOUR BACK-SWING TIME!

BARRETT TAYLOR

BIG HANDS OR SMALL, YOU NEED LEVERAGE

ALTHOUGH LARGE, STRONG HANDS CAN BE AN ASSET TOWARD FIRM GRIPPING AND TAKING A GOOD CUT AT THE BALL, POWER AND CONTROL IN THE GOLF SWING ARE A RESULT MAINLY OF *LEVERAGE*, NOT HAND STRENGTH.

MY OWN HANDS ARE SMALL AND ACTUALLY NOT VERY STRONG. I CREATE LEVERAGE THROUGH MY ARMS AND THE CLUB AS A DIRECT RESULT OF APPLYING PROPER BODY ACTION AND A DELAYED RELEASE OF THE CLUBHEAD. THE HANDS SERVE PRIMARILY AS A CONNECTION BETWEEN THE ARMS AND CLUB.

TAKING the STRAIN OUT OF THE FINISH

A SOUND SWING REQUIRES GOOD BALANCE FROM START TO FINISH. MOST PROS TRY TO REMAIN BALANCED EVEN AFTER THE FINISH, ESPECIALLY ON THE PRACTICE TEE.

... AFTER A HIGH, WELL-BALANCED FINISH WITH WEIGHT ON THE LEFT FOOT, THE PLAYER ASSUMES A MORE NATURAL AND LESS STRAINING POSITION BY LETTING THE CLUB LOWER IN THE GENERAL DIRECTION OF THE HOLE, ALMOST AS A CONTINUED ACTION.

THIS IS TO EXPLAIN WHY THE PROS USE THE SYSTEM, NOT THAT EVERYONE SHOULD, AND TO SHOW THE IMPORTANCE OF BALANCE AND NATURALNESS IN THE MIND OF THE EXPERT.

SMOOTHING OUT THE FINISH

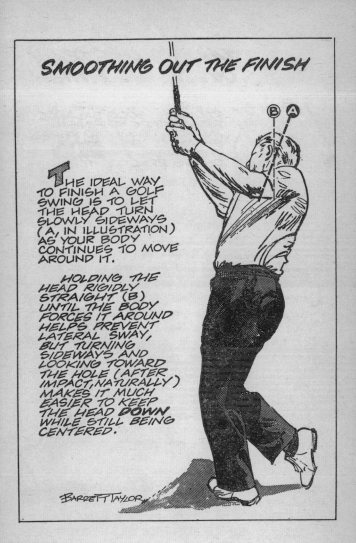

THE IDEAL WAY TO FINISH A GOLF SWING IS TO LET THE HEAD TURN SLOWLY SIDEWAYS (A, IN ILLUSTRATION) AS YOUR BODY CONTINUES TO MOVE AROUND IT.

HOLDING THE HEAD RIGIDLY STRAIGHT (B) UNTIL THE BODY FORCES IT AROUND HELPS PREVENT LATERAL SWAY, BUT TURNING SIDEWAYS AND LOOKING TOWARD THE HOLE (AFTER IMPACT, NATURALLY) MAKES IT MUCH EASIER TO KEEP THE HEAD **DOWN** WHILE STILL BEING CENTERED.

BARRETT TAYLOR

CHAPTER 2

Playing the Course

Unfortunately, golf is not always played under ideal conditions of weather and terrain. Quite often, in fact, the elements prove to be more troublesome than an opponent. Ugly winds may catch a beautifully lofted shot and drop it in a bunker; a perverse rainstorm may have drowned your ball in the fairway; or a careless green-keeper may have forgotten to fill a bare lie, just the spot where your ball picked to land.

These situations are just as frustrating to a professional golfer as they are to a recreational golfer. The one thing we have in common here is that we all must play the ball from where it lies—except, of course, when the rules permit us a free drop from an unplayable lie. But in this section I am concerned with that whole bagful of shots that must be made when the wind is swirling around you or when the terrain confronts you with special hitting problems not covered in your golf primer.

Wind is probably the No. 1 enemy of the average golfer. And the problem is usually compounded by attempting to fight the wind rather than to use it to your advantage. The first rule of driving into the wind is teeing up the ball lower than usual and playing for a low shot; this will enable your ball to bore through the wind, cutting down the chances of its being swept off line and off the fairway. Wind conditions also affect your club choice, and you will find these contingencies covered in the pages ahead.

But don't be fooled by the wind. Often, you see golfers tossing a pinch of grass into the air to gauge the strength and direction of the wind. This often can be very deceiving, for the wind near the ground may not be a true indication of what it is like higher up. The best clues to what your ball will do up in the breezes can be found by checking how the clubhouse flag is blowing or the leaves and branches on top of tall trees. So don't be misled by surface winds. To be sure, look up.

ADJUSTING for WIND

WHEN PLAYING UNDER STRONG WIND CONDITIONS A **WIDER** STANCE HELPS YOU MAINTAIN BALANCE, BUT ALSO SETS UP A RESTRICTION THAT MUST BE COMPENSATED FOR . . .

. . . WIDENING THE STANCE WILL CUT DOWN YOUR BODY TURN AND SHORTEN THE BACKSWING. TO MAKE UP THE RESULTING LOSS OF DISTANCE SIMPLY USE A CLUB LENGTH EXTRA. WHERE YOU WOULD NORMALLY USE A 5 IRON, SELECT A 4.

BRACING YOURSELF THUS, YOU PLAY A PUNCH TYPE OF SHOT. WITH THE SHORTER BACKSWING HIT WELL DOWN ON THE BALL, BUT BE SURE TO KEEP THE SWING SMOOTH AND UNHURRIED.

BARRETT TAYLOR

HITTING into the WIND

FOR BEST CONTROL WHEN PLAYING DIRECTLY INTO THE WIND, THE BALL SHOULD BE HIT LOW WITH A MINIMUM OF BACKSPIN.

THE BEST WAY TO REDUCE BACKSPIN IS TO PLAY THE BALL BACK NEARER THE RIGHT FOOT WHILE KEEPING THE HANDS IN A NORMAL RELATION TO THE BALL. (IF THE BALL IS MOVED BACK 2 INCHES, SO ARE THE HANDS). THIS REQUIRES THAT THE STRAIGHT LINE USUALLY FORMED BY THE LEFT ARM AND CLUB BE ALTERED.

THIS SYSTEM APPLIES TO ALL CLUBS. HOWEVER, ON IRON SHOTS, DROP DOWN TWO OR THREE CLUBS (4, SAY, INSTEAD OF A 6), DEPENDING ON THE STRENGTH OF THE WIND, AND HIT THE SHOT VERY SOFTLY.

BARRETT TAYLOR"

THE BALL WILL START LOW AND STAY LOW.

HEADWIND TACTICS

FOR BEST CONTROL WHEN HITTING INTO WIND, TRY DROPPING DOWN TWO CLUB NUMBERS INSTEAD OF THE CUSTOMARY ONE.

IF THE FLAG IS NORMAL 6 IRON DISTANCE AWAY, RATHER THAN TAKE A CHANCE ON THE BALL "BALLOONING" WITH THE 5 IRON, TAKE A 4 IRON AND HIT **EASY.**

THIS PLACES LESS BACKSPIN ON THE BALL, KEEPS IT LOWER AND THUS MAKES IT BORE BETTER.

...THE SAME APPLIES TO A DRIVE. I'LL TEE LOW AND BACK FARTHER IN MY STANCE, SWING EASY AND SORT OF SLIDE THE BALL THROUGH THE BREEZE.

5 IRON

4 IRON

14

BARRETT TAYLOR

HITTING DOWNWIND

THERE ARE TWO BASIC WAYS TO PLAY DOWN-WIND APPROACH SHOTS. CHOICE DEPENDS SOLELY UPON THE TYPE OF GREEN...

...IT IS SAFEST AND EASIEST TO LET THE BALL LAND SHORT AND ROLL ON, PROVIDING THE FRONT OF THE GREEN IS FREE OF HAZARDS...

...WITH TROUBLE IN FRONT OF A GREEN, THE SHOT MUST BE EXTRA HIGH SO AS TO LAND SOFTLY. ALSO, YOU MUST UTILIZE THE SLOPE OF THE GREEN FOR BEST STOPPAGE. THAT IS, *FADE* WHEN A GREEN SLOPES *LEFT* AND *DRAW* WHEN IT SLOPES *RIGHT.*

BARRETT TAYLOR

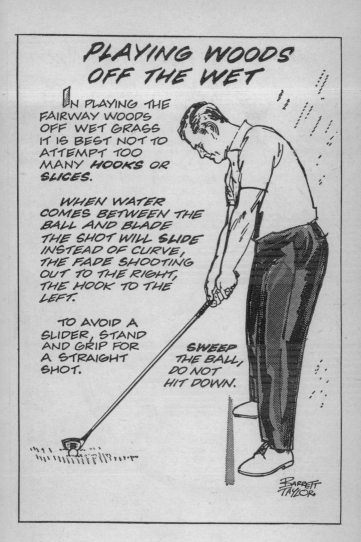

PLAYING WOODS OFF THE WET

IN PLAYING THE FAIRWAY WOODS OFF WET GRASS IT IS BEST NOT TO ATTEMPT TOO MANY **HOOKS** OR **SLICES**.

WHEN WATER COMES BETWEEN THE BALL AND BLADE THE SHOT WILL SLIDE INSTEAD OF CURVE, THE FADE SHOOTING OUT TO THE RIGHT, THE HOOK TO THE LEFT.

TO AVOID A SLIDER, STAND AND GRIP FOR A STRAIGHT SHOT.

SWEEP THE BALL, DO NOT HIT DOWN.

BARRETT TAYLOR.

33

HANDLING WET TURF

TWO PRINCIPLES GOVERN PLAY OFF WET FAIRWAYS. **FIRST**, WATER BETWEEN THE BALL AND CLUB REMOVES BACKSPIN AND MAKES THE SHOT FLY FARTHER. SO USE ONE CLUB HIGHER IN LOFT THAN YOU WOULD NORMALLY.

SECOND, TAKING TURF AFTER HITTING DOWN REDUCES LOFT AND OFTEN INCREASES DISTANCE GAINED TO THAT OF **TWO** CLUBS EXTRA. SO TRY TO **SWEEP** THE BALL CLEANLY.

STRIKE THE BALL AT THE VERY BASE OF YOUR SWING.

BARRETT TAYLOR

DON'T GIVE UP ON A WATERY LIE

HITTING OUT OF SHALLOW WATER IS MUCH LIKE BLASTING FROM A BURIED LIE IN SAND, AND IF THE BALL RESTS ONLY JUST BELOW THE WATER SURFACE WITH NO ROCK OBSTRUCTION OR BLOCKING LEDGE, IT CAN BE PLAYED SUCCESSFULLY.

THE IDEA IS TO SORT OF CUT THE BALL OUT. SO ADDRESS THE SHOT WITH AN OPEN CLUBFACE AND OPEN STANCE, THEN PICK THE CLUB UP ABRUPTLY ON THE BACKSWING.

HIT DOWN SHARPLY AND TRY TO CATCH AS MUCH OF THE BALL AS POSSIBLE. LET THE CLUBHEAD GO DEEP INTO THE MUD OR SAND AFTER IMPACT.

BARRETT TAYLOR

35

HITTING WOODS FROM BARE LIES

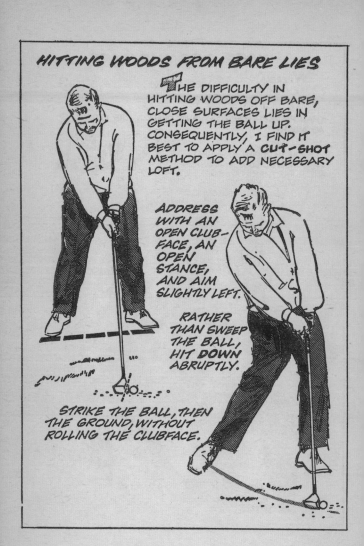

THE DIFFICULTY IN HITTING WOODS OFF BARE, CLOSE SURFACES LIES IN GETTING THE BALL UP. CONSEQUENTLY, I FIND IT BEST TO APPLY A **CUT-SHOT** METHOD TO ADD NECESSARY LOFT.

ADDRESS WITH AN OPEN CLUB-FACE, AN OPEN STANCE, AND AIM SLIGHTLY LEFT.

RATHER THAN SWEEP THE BALL, HIT **DOWN** ABRUPTLY.

STRIKE THE BALL, THEN THE GROUND, WITHOUT ROLLING THE CLUBFACE.

HARD GROUND LIES

WHEREAS I TRY TO SWEEP, OR PICK, THE BALL OFF FROZEN GROUND, FROM ORDINARY *HARD* GROUND MY TECHNIQUE IS JUST THE OPPOSITE — I HIT *DOWN* ON THE BALL. I FIND THAT HARD OFFERS LESS RESISTANCE THAN FROZEN, HENCE DOESN'T DEFLECT THE CLUBHEAD AS MUCH.

FROM HARDPAN THE BALL WILL TRAVEL LOWER AND RUN MUCH FARTHER THAN USUAL. TO COMPENSATE FOR THIS AND TO HOLD THE GREEN YOU MUST PUT EXCESS SPIN ON THE BALL...

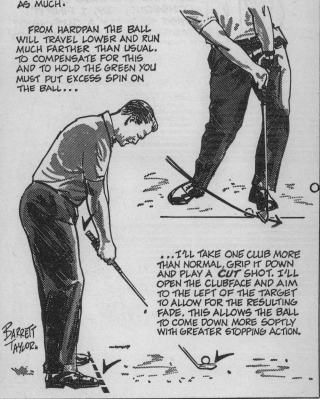

...I'LL TAKE ONE CLUB MORE THAN NORMAL, GRIP IT DOWN AND PLAY A *CUT* SHOT. I'LL OPEN THE CLUBFACE AND AIM TO THE LEFT OF THE TARGET TO ALLOW FOR THE RESULTING FADE. THIS ALLOWS THE BALL TO COME DOWN MORE SOFTLY WITH GREATER STOPPING ACTION.

BARRETT TAYLOR

GETTING DISTANCE FROM HEAVY LIES

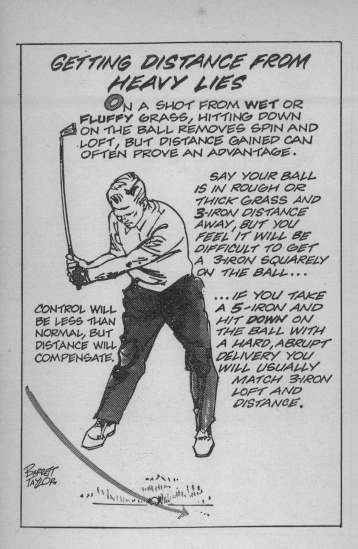

ON A SHOT FROM **WET** OR **FLUFFY** GRASS, HITTING DOWN ON THE BALL REMOVES SPIN AND LOFT, BUT DISTANCE GAINED CAN OFTEN PROVE AN ADVANTAGE.

SAY YOUR BALL IS IN ROUGH OR THICK GRASS AND 3-IRON DISTANCE AWAY, BUT YOU FEEL IT WILL BE DIFFICULT TO GET A 3-IRON SQUARELY ON THE BALL...

...IF YOU TAKE A 5-IRON AND HIT DOWN ON THE BALL WITH A HARD, ABRUPT DELIVERY YOU WILL USUALLY MATCH 3-IRON LOFT AND DISTANCE.

CONTROL WILL BE LESS THAN NORMAL, BUT DISTANCE WILL COMPENSATE.

BARRETT TAYLOR

PITCHING from GRASSY LIES

WHEN THE BALL LIES IN A *GRASSY BANK* NEAR THE GREEN'S EDGE, PLAY IT AS FOLLOWS:

1 USUALLY THE BALL WILL BE SITTING UP FAIRLY WELL, SO LET THE SWING FOLLOW THE GENERAL SLOPE OF THE BANK — THAT IS, *SWEEP* THE BALL UP. THIS BRINGS IT OUT SOFTLY AND STOPS IT QUICKLY. SWING HARDER THAN IS NORMAL TO COMPENSATE FOR A HIGHER TRAJECTORY.

BARRETT TAYLOR

2 THE SWEEPING METHOD LESSENS THE COMMON TENDENCY TO STICK THE CLUB IN THE GROUND BEHIND THE BALL. HOWEVER, IF THE BALL IS IN A **HOLE**, THERE IS NO CHOICE BUT TO HIT RIGHT INTO THE BANK. OPEN THE CLUBFACE AND SWING ALMOST AS IF THE LIE WERE *FLAT.* BE SURE TO STRIKE THE BALL FIRST.

PITCHING FROM THICK LIES

A DELICATE SHOT THAT MIGHT CONFRONT YOU OCCASIONALLY IS THE SHORT PITCH SHOT FROM THICK SPONGY GRASS.

THOUGH THE BALL SITS UP WELL, EXTRA CARE MUST BE TAKEN TO AVOID SCOOPING UNDER IT.

FOR A SHOT THAT NORMALLY CALLS FOR AN 8 OR A 9 IRON, I PREFER TO USE THE WEDGE AND SORT OF *SWEEP* THE BALL, CATCHING IT ON THE UPSWING...

...THIS INSURES A MORE SOLID CONTACT THAN IS POSSIBLE THROUGH HITTING DOWN (*SHOWN RIGHT*) IN THE NORMAL WAY, AND PROVIDES BETTER CONTROL. IT PRODUCES A "DEAD" BALL THAT TRAVELS HIGH, LANDS GENTLY AND STOPS QUICKLY.

BARRETT TAYLOR

CHIPPING OUT OF ROUGH

HERE FIRMNESS OF GRIP IS A MUST TO PREVENT GRASS FROM CATCHING THE CLUBHEAD AND CLOSING THE FACE THROUGH IMPACT.

STAYING FIRM, HOWEVER, DOES NOT MEAN ADDRESSING THE BALL WITH A VISE-LIKE GRIP AND DELIVERING A QUICK, CHOPPY SWING.

GRIP ONLY AS YOU WOULD NORMALLY AND EXECUTE A SMOOTH, DELIBERATE SWING.

TO KEEP THE CLUBFACE SQUARE AND ACCELERATING TOWARD THE HOLE, FIRM UP SLIGHTLY WITH YOUR RIGHT HAND JUST BEFORE STRIKING THE BALL.

GETTING BITE out of ROUGH

ALTHOUGH PUTTING BITE, OR BACKSPIN, ON A BALL OUT OF ROUGH IS DIFFICULT, IT CAN BE DONE PROVIDING THE LIE IS FAIRLY GOOD WITH THE BALL SITTING GENERALLY ON TOP OF THE GRASS.

TO PRODUCE BACKSPIN THE CLUB MUST COME DOWN ON THE BALL AT A VERY STEEP ANGLE— IN A SLICING, NOT HOOKING, FASHION.

THE CLUBFACE IS OPENED SLIGHTLY AT ADDRESS AND IS PICKED UP VERY ABRUPTLY ON THE BACKSWING. IT CONTACTS THE BALL BEFORE MUCH GRASS CAN INTERFERE, SENDING THE BALL HIGH WITH BACKSPIN.

BARRETT TAYLOR

HITTING OFF LOOSE OBJECTS

1 IF YOUR BALL STOPS ON TWIGS, LEAVES OR PINE NEEDLES, TAKE CARE NOT TO GROUND YOUR CLUB OR TRY TO REMOVE ANY SCRAPS. ONE PARTICLE MAY BE CONNECTED TO ANOTHER AND TRIGGER OFF BALL MOVEMENT AND PENALTY.

ON FULL SHOTS THE BALL WILL USUALLY COME OFF WELL, SO SWING NORMALLY.

AROUND THE GREEN LOOSE STUFF WILL REACT LIKE SAND, SO PLAY IT LIKE A BLAST. HIT ABOUT ½" OR 1" BEHIND THE BALL USING YOUR SAND WEDGE.

BARRETT TAYLOR

STOPPING the BALL WITHOUT BACKSPIN

THERE ARE TWO WAYS TO HOLD THE GREEN ON SHOTS FROM ROUGH: APPLYING BACKSPIN—A TOUGH JOB AT BEST—OR PLAYING THE *LOB* SHOT.

THIS SHOT IS PLAYED WITH A SWEEPING TYPE SWING THAT STRIKES THE BACK OF THE BALL, SENDING IT HIGH WITH VERY LITTLE BACKSPIN.

SINCE THE BALL WILL FLY FARTHER FROM ROUGH, COMPENSATE BY USING ONE CLUB SHORTER THAN NORMALLY CALLED FOR. (WHEN 9-IRON DISTANCE AWAY, CHOOSE A WEDGE.) SINCE THE BALL WILL FLY HIGHER AND LAND MORE SOFTLY, IT WILL STOP MORE QUICKLY.

ATTEMPT THIS SHOT ONLY FROM A FAIRLY GOOD LIE ATOP THE ROUGH.

BARRETT TAYLOR

CHAPTER 3

Strategy and Trouble Shots

How many times have you heard it said: "You don't play your opponent, you play the course"? This is true. The course is your most formidable opponent every time, and you must look for places to beat it, find out where it is most vulnerable. You don't play winning golf simply by standing on the tee, sighting the flag, and then blasting away. You must learn to play the course the way it is laid out.

This chapter, therefore, is broken down into two sections. The first deals with the various ways there are in sizing up a golf course; the second covers the means of executing some of the trouble shots you'll run into, such as hitting from downhill or sidehill lies or hitting over obstructions like trees and hillocks.

The most important first step you can take is finding the correct location for teeing up your ball. Many players feel that when the green opening is on the right side, they should position the ball on the right side of the tee. This theory is true to a certain extent. But as you get near the ends of tee areas you will often find uneven slopes—and they should be avoided. It's far more important to hit the ball solidly from a well-balanced stance on level ground, so in looking for a good tee position, first find as flat a lie as possible. Then worry about your position.

Familiarizing yourself with a course you're playing for the first time is another good way of avoiding trouble in advance. Of course, you don't always have the luxury of walking around a golf course before you play it—as we pros do—but there are instances when you can look ahead. Before hitting an approach to the green, it's a good idea to pace off the distance of the shot you will need; it will firm up in your mind the proper club to use.

There is no instance in golf where a little preplanning and preparedness won't give you an extra edge.

AN IMPORTANT PART OF STRATEGY

Prior to driving, a golfer can save strokes merely by **LOOKING DOWN THE FAIRWAY.** By observing ground slope he can note the advantages or disadvantages presented and play accordingly.

THIS SITUATION OFFERS A NATURAL ADVANTAGE FOR A PLAYED HOOK ———

— HERE, A FADE IS NECESSARY TO HOLD THE FAIRWAY.

AIM RIGHT HERE ——— EVEN IF DRIVE LANDS AMONG SMALL TREES SLOPE WILL USUALLY HELP THE BALL RUN DOWN AND THROUGH.

THESE ARE JUST 3 OF MANY SITUATIONS WHERE SLOPE-CONSCIOUSNESS PAYS.

BARRETT TAYLOR

AVOIDING TROUBLE from THE TEE

—DRIVER

—3 WOOD

B. TAYLOR

WHENEVER YOU RUN INTO A TIGHT SITUATION WHERE DISTANCE ISN'T NECESSARY, BUT WHERE ACCURACY IS AT A PREMIUM, IT IS SIMPLE LOGIC TO USE A 2 OR 3 WOOD FROM THE TEE IN LIEU OF A DRIVER.

HOWEVER, THE SHORTER CLUBS CAN BE USED TO AN ADVANTAGE EVEN IF ACCURACY ISN'T AT PREMIUM, BUT THERE IS SOMETHING YOU WANT TO STAY SHORT OF.

LET'S SAY THERE ARE TWO BIG TREES OUT ON THE RIGHT THAT, 9 TIMES OUT OF 10, WOULD NEVER BOTHER YOU. IF YOU HIT A DRIVER, YOU'RE LIKELY TO BE RIGHT BEHIND THEM THAT ONE TIME — BUT IF YOU TAKE A 3 WOOD AND GET BEHIND THEM, YOU'LL STILL BE FAR ENOUGH BEHIND TO BE ABLE TO FADE AROUND THEM WITH EASE.

THINK AHEAD

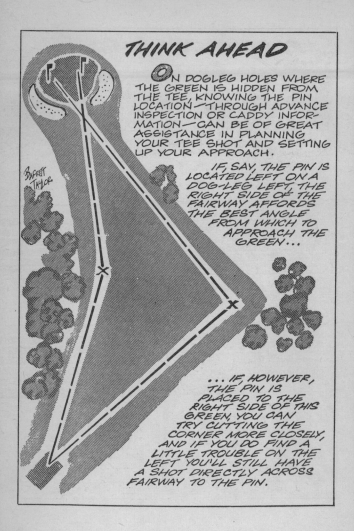

ON DOGLEG HOLES WHERE THE GREEN IS HIDDEN FROM THE TEE, KNOWING THE PIN LOCATION—THROUGH ADVANCE INSPECTION OR CADDY INFORMATION—CAN BE OF GREAT ASSISTANCE IN PLANNING YOUR TEE SHOT AND SETTING UP YOUR APPROACH.

IF, SAY, THE PIN IS LOCATED LEFT ON A DOG-LEG LEFT, THE RIGHT SIDE OF THE FAIRWAY AFFORDS THE BEST ANGLE FROM WHICH TO APPROACH THE GREEN...

...IF, HOWEVER, THE PIN IS PLACED TO THE RIGHT SIDE OF THIS GREEN, YOU CAN TRY CUTTING THE CORNER MORE CLOSELY, AND IF YOU DO FIND A LITTLE TROUBLE ON THE LEFT YOU'LL STILL HAVE A SHOT DIRECTLY ACROSS FAIRWAY TO THE PIN.

BARRETT
TAYLOR

PLAYING DOG-LEGS

CUTTING CORNERS OF DOG-LEG HOLES CAN SHORTEN THEM CONSIDERABLY, AND IF YOUR ABILITY WITH A DRIVER MATCHES YOUR DESIRE FOR AN EASIER 2ND SHOT, THERE IS NO REASON TO TAKE THE LONG ROUTE.

THERE IS, HOWEVER, A TACTICAL PROCEDURE TO FOLLOW... ALWAYS TRY TO PLAY THE BALL TO FOLLOW THE CONTOUR OF THE FAIRWAY. THAT IS, **FADE** TO A DOG-LEG-RIGHT AND **HOOK** TO A DOG-LEG-LEFT. (IF YOU NATURALLY HOOK OR SLICE, NEVER TRY TO CUT THE CORNER OF A HOLE THAT BENDS THE OPPOSITE WAY.)

IN SHORT, WHETHER YOU PLAY SAFELY OR BOLDLY TRY TO BEND THE BALL WITH THE FAIRWAY— IF YOUR ABILITY PERMITS.

BARRETT TAYLOR

CONTROLLING the BALL

ALMOST WITHOUT EXCEPTION, I WILL TRY TO PLAY THE BALL FROM *LEFT-TO-RIGHT* OR FROM *RIGHT-TO-LEFT* WITH EVERY CLUB IN THE BAG. RATHER THAN TRY TO HIT A STRAIGHT SHOT, WHICH IS DIFFICULT TO DO SUCCESSFULLY, I WILL AIM FOR ONE SIDE OF THE FAIRWAY AND TRY TO MOVE THE BALL TO THE MIDDLE. I FIND I CAN MOVE THE BALL EITHER RIGHT OR LEFT WITH SUCCESS 85% OF THE TIME.

IF THERE IS TROUBLE ON THE LEFT SIDE OF THE FAIRWAY, I WILL AIM TO THE LEFT AND FADE THE BALL (LEFT-TO-RIGHT) TO THE MIDDLE, AWAY FROM THE DANGER.

I PREFER TO PLAY THE BALL FROM LEFT-TO-RIGHT, SINCE I AM THE MOST ACCURATE WITH A FADE. BUT IF THERE IS TROUBLE ON THE RIGHT, AND NONE ON THE LEFT, I WILL AIM TO THE RIGHT AND TRY TO HOOK THE BALL SLIGHTLY. (RIGHT-TO-LEFT)

ALLOWING A MARGIN FOR ERROR

I ALWAYS ALLOW A *MARGIN FOR ERROR* IN PLAYING AN APPROACH SHOT TO THE GREEN.

FOR EXAMPLE, IF THE PIN IS ON THE *RIGHT* SIDE, I WILL AIM TO THE CENTER OF THE GREEN AND ATTEMPT TO *FADE* THE BALL SLIGHTLY TO THE HOLE. IF THE BALL HAPPENS TO GO STRAIGHT, I HAVE STILL AVOIDED GOING TO THE LEFT OR OFF THE RIGHT SIDE OF THE GREEN.

LIKEWISE, IF THE PIN IS ON THE *LEFT,* I WILL AIM FOR THE CENTER OF THE GREEN AND TRY TO WORK THE BALL IN WITH A SLIGHT *DRAW.*

I NEVER TRY TO HIT A *STRAIGHT* BALL WITH THE LONG CLUBS. ON RARE OCCASIONS, WHEN FACTORS PERMIT, I WILL ATTEMPT TO HIT THE SHOT STRAIGHT, BUT WITH NO LONGER A CLUB THAN A 5-IRON. I FIND I CAN BE STRAIGHT WITH THE 5, 6, 7, 8, 9, AND WEDGE MOST OF THE TIME.

HOWEVER, CONDITIONS GENERALLY NECESSITATE FADING OR DRAWING A SHOT.

WHEN TO GAMBLE

Often a gamble is not so much of a gamble if the situation is analized with good judgement.

On a recovery shot I try to *gamble* as much as possible—without being foolish.

If I am confronted by a few trees, and I see little additional trouble around, I will try to work the ball through the trees. If I hit one, I will usually have as good a third shot as if I had chipped out safely; and very possibly I may land on or near the green.

Of course, if you are in a *dense* forest or there is water or out-of-bounds nearby, you don't dare gamble.

I concentrate upon the *result I want from the shot,* not upon any trouble that might occur.

B. TAYLOR

WHEN SAFETY PAYS

IN STROKE PLAY, WHEN WINNING DOES NOT DEPEND UPON ANY ONE SHOT, IT'S BEST TO PLAY AWAY FROM DANGER. MANY A GOOD ROUND HAS BEEN SPOILED BY A RISKY SHOT THAT FAILED.

DURING THE '61 NATIONAL OPEN, I MISSED MY APPROACH AT 18. TO RECOVER CLOSE TO THE PIN ENTAILED A VERY DELICATE SHOT OVER A DEEP, WIDE TRAP AND A MOUND (A).

RESISTING TEMPTATION, I CHOSE TO PLAY WELL BEYOND THE DANGER BY MEANS OF A HIGH, SOFT WEDGE SHOT (B). THIS LEFT A 15 FOOT PUTT WHICH, INCIDENTALLY, I ALMOST SANK.

HAD I GAMBLED AND CAUGHT THE TRAP, I COULD HAVE TAKEN A 6 OR 7. AS IT TURNED OUT, I PRESERVED A TIE FOR 4TH IN THE TOURNAMENT.

BARRETT TAYLOR

TEE SHOTS WITH A PURPOSE

NEVER BE CONTENT MERELY TO HIT THE FAIRWAY, WIDE AS IT MAY BE, BUT ALWAYS STRIVE TO *PINPOINT* YOUR DRIVE.

MOST GOLF HOLES ARE SO DESIGNED THAT A SPECIFIC SIDE OR PORTION OF THE FAIRWAY AFFORDS THE MOST FAVORABLE POSITION FROM WHICH TO HIT THE APPROACH.

THIS IS TRUE OF YOUR OWN HOME LAYOUT AS WELL AS SUCH FAMOUS COURSES AS THE AUGUSTA NATIONAL, WHERE A DRIVE TO THE WRONG SIDE OF THOSE WIDE FAIRWAYS CAN MAKE SCORING EXTREMELY DIFFICULT.

STUDY THIS HOLE AS AN EXAMPLE: HERE THE DRIVE SHOULD BE PLACED RIGHT, FROM WHERE AN APPROACH, EVEN OUT OF ROUGH, IS PREFERABLE TO A POSITION LEFT.

BARRETT TAYLOR

CHOOSING A TARGET

THE SUCCESS OF ANY APPROACH SHOT RESTS LARGELY ON CHOICE OF TARGET, OR AIMING POINT.

PERSONALLY, I DO NOT AIM FOR ANY PARTICULAR PORTION OF THE GREEN ITSELF. MY TARGET MUST BE A DEFINITE, WELL DEFINED OBJECT OR LANDMARK...

... IT IS USUALLY THE *PIN*. BUT IF IT IS TUCKED BACK BEHIND A HAZARD, MAKING A DIRECT SHOT DANGEROUS, THEN THE EDGE OF A TRAP OR A MOUND MAY BECOME THE TARGET.

...IT MAY BE A TREE BEHIND THE GREEN TOWARD WHICH I MAY AIM, THEN FADE OR HOOK THE BALL IN TO THE HOLE.

THE BASIC THOUGHT IS TO FOCUS THE EYE ON SOMETHING PROMINENT, NOT VAGUE.

USE 3 WOOD for POSITION

THE MAIN REASON FOR USING A 3 WOOD INSTEAD OF A DRIVER FROM THE TEE IS NOT DIRECTION, BUT *POSITION*... TO AFFORD A BETTER APPROACH ANGLE FOR THE SECOND SHOT. USE IT WHEN YOU WANT TO STAY WITHIN A WIDE SECTION OF THE FAIRWAY, OR TO STAY SHORT OF TREES, TRAPS WATER, ETC...

DRIVER

3 WOOD

...IN MOST CASES A GOLFER WILL HIT A DRIVER JUST AS STRAIGHT AS A 3 WOOD, BUT THE IDEA OF HITTING THE DRIVER EASY DOESN'T ALWAYS WORK...

...A FULLY POWERED 3 WOOD IS MOST NATURAL AND ACCURATE FOR STAYING SHORT OF TROUBLE.

BARRETT TAYLOR

PICK AN AREA TO HIT, NOT AVOID

Positive thinking certainly produces better golf than negative, particularly in aiming the shot.

I always select a definite spot, or landmark, as a target. It may be an area near the edge of a trap or adjacent to a group of trees. I will then try to work the ball in to the fairway by hooking or fading the ball away from these landmarks...

... I try to expel all fear of the hazard and the trouble that could possibly result from a slight miscue...

... think only of the results you seek, then swing freely toward your target.

HITTING OVER TREES

BLOCKING TREES ARE SELDOM THE INSURMOUNTABLE BARRIERS THEY SEEM, FOR EVEN A NORMAL SWING WILL RAISE THE BALL HIGHER AND MORE QUICKLY THAN MOST WEEKENDERS WOULD SUPPOSE.

BARRETT TAYLOR

FOR MAXIMUM LOFT, OPEN THE CLUBFACE SLIGHTLY AT ADDRESS AND ALLOW FOR A FADE.

THE MAIN THING IS TO STAY WELL BEHIND THE SHOT BY KEEPING THE HEAD STEADY AND BRINGING THE RIGHT SHOULDER FAR UNDER THROUGH THE HIT, WHILE DELIVERING A BIT MORE RIGHT HAND TO GET UNDER THE BALL.

PLAYING BLIND HOLES

THE TWO OBVIOUS PROBLEMS IN HITTING TO A FLAG BEHIND A HILL ARE KNOWING HOW FAR TO HIT AND WHERE TO HIT. BOTH CAN BE SOLVED BY WALKING TO THE CREST...

...NOTE THE DISTANCE TO THE GREEN, THEN ADD THE DISTANCE BACK TO THE BALL...

...FOR A TARGET, SELECT A TREE OR ANY TALL OBJECT IN THE AREA DIRECTLY BEHIND THE PIN...

...KEEP AN EYE ON THIS MARKER AS YOU WALK BACK TO THE BALL SO AS NOT TO LOSE IT.

BARRETT TAYLOR

50 YDS.   60 YDS.

TOTAL: 110 YDS.

TAKE A TIP from THE TERRAIN

AT TIMES YOU MAY ENCOUNTER THE CONFUSING SITUATION WHERE THE BREAK OF A PUTT APPEARS TO DIFFER GREATLY WHEN VIEWED FROM OPPOSITE SIDES OF THE HOLE. IN THIS CASE, THE *SURROUNDING TERRAIN* WILL OFTEN REVEAL THE TRUE LINE. YOU'LL FIND THE BALL MOST LIKELY TO TURN *WITH* THE GENERAL SLOPE OF THE LAND THAN *AGAINST* IT. SO WHEN IN DOUBT, *LOOK AROUND!*

SURROUNDING AREA INDICATES *SOLID* LINE MOST LIKELY TO BE CORRECT.

BARRETT TAYLOR

The DOWNHILL LIE

THE BEST WAY TO AVOID A STEEP DOWNHILL LIE IS TO PLAY AROUND IT, BUT IF THE PROBLEM ARISES, SOLVE IT THUS:

PLAY BALL *FARTHER BACK* TOWARD RIGHT FOOT WITH *OPEN* STANCE AND MOST OF WEIGHT TO THE *LEFT*.

SHOT WILL TRAVEL LOW SO USE ONE CLUB HIGHER THAN NORMALLY NEEDED. OPEN BLADE TO AVOID PULLING, THEN TAKE AN *UPRIGHT* BACKSWING, BREAKING WRISTS VERY *SHARPLY*.

HIT VERY HARD AT IMPACT, BUT KEEP WRISTS FROM ROLLING AS THE CLUBHEAD MOVES LOW TOWARD THE TARGET.

BARRETT TAYLOR.

UPHILL LIES

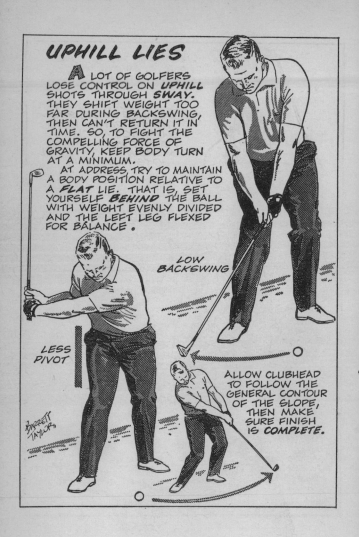

A LOT OF GOLFERS LOSE CONTROL ON *UPHILL* SHOTS THROUGH *SWAY.* THEY SHIFT WEIGHT TOO FAR DURING BACKSWING, THEN CAN'T RETURN IT IN TIME. SO, TO FIGHT THE COMPELLING FORCE OF GRAVITY, KEEP BODY TURN AT A MINIMUM.

AT ADDRESS, TRY TO MAINTAIN A BODY POSITION RELATIVE TO A *FLAT* LIE. THAT IS, SET YOURSELF *BEHIND* THE BALL WITH WEIGHT EVENLY DIVIDED AND THE LEFT LEG FLEXED FOR BALANCE.

LOW BACKSWING

LESS PIVOT

BARRETT TAYLOR

ALLOW CLUBHEAD TO FOLLOW THE GENERAL CONTOUR OF THE SLOPE, THEN MAKE SURE FINISH IS *COMPLETE.*

HITTING DOWNHILL

UPSLOPES, LIKE DOWNSLOPES, PRESENT BALANCE PROBLEMS. THE TENDENCY IS TO SHIFT TOO MUCH WEIGHT DURING THE BACKSWING ON UPHILL SHOTS AND NOT ENOUGH ON DOWNHILL SHOTS.

SOUNDS OPPOSED TO BASICS, BUT YOU CAN OFFSET THE EFFECT OF DOWNHILL GRAVITY BY PLACING MOST OF YOUR WEIGHT ON YOUR RIGHT FOOT AT ADDRESS, THEN IT WILL ALREADY BE THERE WHEN YOU REACH THE TOP OF THE BACKSWING. ACTUALLY, VERY LITTLE BODY ACTION IS NECESSARY ON THIS TYPE OF SHOT.

DOWNHILL, YOU MUST APPLY EXTRA HAND ACTION IN ORDER TO GET THE CLUBFACE UNDER THE BALL. UPHILL, YOU NEED MORE ARM ACCENT FOR THE SAME REASON.

WRISTS

ARMS

BARRETT TAYLOR

The DOWNHILL PITCH

THE MOST IMPORTANT THING IN PITCHING FROM DOWNHILL LIES — AND ONE WHICH REQUIRES EFFORT BEYOND THAT FOR A NORMAL PITCH — IS TO STRIKE THE BALL *FIRST.*

MY METHOD OF MEETING THIS REQUIREMENT IS TO STAY WELL AHEAD OF THE SHOT AND HIT VERY HARD WITH MY *RIGHT HAND...*

...I TRY TO CUT *UNDER* THE BALL A LITTLE IN ORDER TO GRIP THE BALL FIRMLY ON THE CLUBFACE, USING A LOW, EXTENDED FOLLOW-THROUGH.

SINCE LOFT WILL BE REDUCED FROM NORMAL, USE ONE CLUB HIGHER THAN USUAL (WEDGE INSTEAD OF A 9).

BARRETT TAYLOR

FROM _____

ADDRESS _____

CITY _____ STATE _____ ZIP _____

BUSINESS REPLY CARD

NO POSTAGE NECESSARY IF MAILED IN THE UNITED STATES

1255 PORTLAND PLACE
BOULDER, COLO. 80302

FIRST CLASS

Permit No. 486
Boulder, Colo.

PITCHING FROM A HIGH SIDEHILL LIE

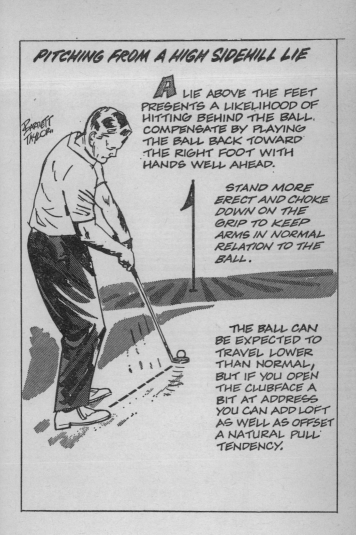

A LIE ABOVE THE FEET PRESENTS A LIKELIHOOD OF HITTING BEHIND THE BALL. COMPENSATE BY PLAYING THE BALL BACK TOWARD THE RIGHT FOOT WITH HANDS WELL AHEAD.

STAND MORE ERECT AND CHOKE DOWN ON THE GRIP TO KEEP ARMS IN NORMAL RELATION TO THE BALL.

THE BALL CAN BE EXPECTED TO TRAVEL LOWER THAN NORMAL, BUT IF YOU OPEN THE CLUBFACE A BIT AT ADDRESS YOU CAN ADD LOFT AS WELL AS OFFSET A NATURAL PULL TENDENCY.

BARRETT TAYLOR

CHIPPING FROM A LOW SIDEHILL LIE

CHIPPING A BALL BELOW THE FEET REQUIRES SEVERAL ADJUSTMENTS IN SWING AND STANCE TO OFFSET A NATURAL PUSH TENDENCY AND REDUCTION OF LOFT.

ADDRESS THE BALL FARTHER BACK NEAR THE RIGHT FOOT WITH A VERY OPEN STANCE AND THE HANDS WELL AHEAD OF THE BALL TO HELP PREVENT HITTING 'FAT.'

CUT ACROSS THE BALL BY MEANS OF A PRONOUNCED OUTSIDE-IN SWING...

...THEN DIRECT THE FOLLOW THROUGH LEFT, ALMOST DIRECTLY UP THE SLOPE. THE OPEN FACE WILL SEND THE BALL OFF TO THE RIGHT TOWARD THE HOLE.

The HALF-IN, HALF-OUT BLAST

THERE IS NO NEED FOR ANXIETY IF A BALL RESTS ON SAND SPILL NEAR A TRAP'S EDGE. LOGICALLY, IT'S AN EASY SHOT, EVEN LESS COMPLICATED THAN A NORMAL BLAST.

.. NORMALLY, IT IS QUITE CRITICAL TO HIT EXACTLY THE RIGHT DEPTH INTO SAND IN ORDER TO PROVIDE THE CLUB-HEAD BOUNCE NEEDED TO GET UNDER THE BALL...

...BUT IN THIS INSTANCE, THE GROUND *BELOW* THE LIGHT LAYER OF SAND PROVIDES THE BOUNCE, SERVING AS A FIRM BASE TO PREVENT DIGGING TOO DEEPLY.

USE YOUR SAND WEDGE AND PLAY IT JUST LIKE A NORMAL SAND SHOT, HITTING A COUPLE OF INCHES BEHIND THE BALL.

SAND

EARTH

BARRETT TAYLOR

RECOVERING from A BAD SHOT

FOLLOWING A "MISSED" SHOT, THE MAIN TASK IS TO CURB FRUSTRATION AND AVOID REPEATING THE ERROR...

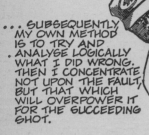

... SUBSEQUENTLY MY OWN METHOD IS TO TRY AND ANALYSE LOGICALLY WHAT I DID WRONG. THEN I CONCENTRATE NOT UPON THE FAULT, BUT THAT WHICH WILL OVERPOWER IT FOR THE SUCCEEDING SHOT.

FOR INSTANCE, IF I DEDUCE THAT A TENSING OF THE RIGHT ARM CAUSED THE ERROR, I WILL STRIVE TO OFFSET THIS WITH FIRMER LEFT ARM OR LEFT SIDE CONTROL.

IN OTHER WORDS, USE A *POSITIVE*, RATHER THAN A NEGATIVE, APPROACH. CATER NOT TO THE FAULT, BUT TO THE REMEDY.

BARRETT TAYLOR

CHAPTER 4

First-Aid on the Course

When your game suddenly goes sour out on the course, you can't very well summon your professional, as you would your physician in a midnight emergency. In such cases, a few home remedies are called for—a golfer's first-aid, so to speak.

The symptoms and illnesses I'm talking about here have to do with such unmentionables as hooks, slices, scuffs, and tops, any of which can creep into your game when you least expect it. The important point is not to delude yourself when it begins to happen. If you've pulled two shots in a row into the woods, obviously something drastic has occurred, and the time to analyze what you are doing wrong and how to correct it is right then and there. Otherwise, you may compound your mistakes.

While I'll deal more graphically with some of the more vexing problems that befall even low-handicap players in the course of this chapter, let me capsulize a few of the common ones here.

Both the hook and the slice are caused by hitting from the top. In the hook, you probably have rolled your shoulders just before impact, causing the left hand to pull in from the intended line of flight and resulting in a duck hook. In the slice, you may have relaxed your grip at the top, taken an open stance, and made your downswing on an outside-in path. The topped shot has many causes, the most common of which is placing the ball exactly in the center of your stance at address; this prevents you from getting your weight properly behind the shot, with the result that your clubhead swings over the ball. The ugly shank comes from addressing the ball with your weight pressed in toward your toes and your arms less than fully extended; thus, you wind up cutting across the ball, and more often than not, striking the ball with the hosel of your club.

When errors crop up in your game, pausing for a little self-analysis could make a big difference.

LOOK OUT for LAG

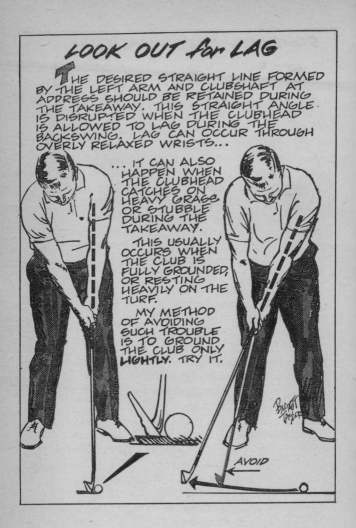

THE DESIRED STRAIGHT LINE FORMED BY THE LEFT ARM AND CLUBSHAFT AT ADDRESS SHOULD BE RETAINED DURING THE TAKEAWAY. THIS STRAIGHT ANGLE IS DISRUPTED WHEN THE CLUBHEAD IS ALLOWED TO LAG DURING THE BACKSWING. LAG CAN OCCUR THROUGH OVERLY RELAXED WRISTS...

... IT CAN ALSO HAPPEN WHEN THE CLUBHEAD CATCHES ON HEAVY GRASS OR STUBBLE DURING THE TAKEAWAY.

THIS USUALLY OCCURS WHEN THE CLUB IS FULLY GROUNDED, OR RESTING HEAVILY ON THE TURF.

MY METHOD OF AVOIDING SUCH TROUBLE IS TO GROUND THE CLUB ONLY **LIGHTLY**. TRY IT.

AVOID

STEADY RIGHT LEG VITAL

FOR A BALANCED SWING THE **RIGHT LEG** MUST STAY FIXED ALL DURING THE BACKSWING.

THE LEG IS FLEXED SLIGHTLY AT THE ADDRESS AND REMAINS SO.

RIGHT LEG MUST NOT **SWAY** RIGHT OR LEFT.

IF THE RIGHT LEG **COLLAPSES** GOING BACK YOU WILL FIND DIFFICULTY IN SHIFTING WEIGHT **LEFT** ON THE DOWNSWING. A SLICE OR 'FAT' HIT MAY RESULT.

A **LOCKED**, STRAIGHT LEG ALSO RESTRICTS SHIFT AND MAY CAUSE YOU TO HIT ON THE **UP-SWING**.

BARRETT TAYLOR

YOU and YOUR SHADOW

"ME AND MY SHADOW" TOGETHER SOLVE A LOT OF SWAY PROBLEMS— YOU AND YOURS CAN DO THE SAME.

OFTEN, WHEN THE SUN IS RIGHT DURING PRACTICE, I WILL TAKE ADVANTAGE OF MY CAST SILHOUETTE TO CHECK MY SWING, ESPECIALLY HEAD POSITION.

BEING BELOW THE HORIZON, THIS IMAGE CAN BE STUDIED EASILY WHILE THE HEAD REMAINS IN A NATURAL POSITION.

IF YOU ALIGN THE EDGE OF YOUR HEAD SHADOW WITH AN OBJECT, LIKE A TALL BLADE OF GRASS, ANY SLIGHT LATERAL MOTION OF THE HEAD WILL BE READILY APPARENT.

BARRETT TAYLOR

(SWING AT AN EMPTY TEE OR A WEED—NOT A BALL)

WATCH YOUR LOOP

I ALWAYS TRY TO TAKE THE CLUB STRAIGHT BACK ON A LINE PARALLEL WITH THE TARGET, THEN TRY TO MAKE THE DOWNSWING FOLLOW THE SAME ARC AS THE BACKSWING. I DON'T KNOW IF I ACTUALLY RETURN THE CLUB ON THE SAME PATH, BUT THAT IS HOW IT *FEELS* TO ME, AND HAS ALWAYS BEEN ONE OF MY *CHECKPOINTS* WHEN I'M PULLING OR PUSHING MY SHOTS.

ACTUALLY, IT IS DIFFICULT TO KEEP THE SWING PATH, OR ARC, OF THE DOWNSWING EXACTLY THE SAME AS THAT OF THE BACKSWING BECAUSE THE HIPS ASSUME A DIFFERENT POSITION AS THE WEIGHT SHIFTS TO THE LEFT ON THE DOWNSWING. THIS TENDS TO PRODUCE A SLIGHT *LOOPING* OF THE CLUB AS THE DOWNSWING BEGINS.

LOOP SHOULD COME FROM INSIDE

LOOP SHOULD NEVER COME FROM OUTSIDE!

B. TAYLOR.

EVEN THE EXPERT GOLFER MAY HAVE A SLIGHT LOOP. HOWEVER, THE LOOP SHOULD ALWAYS COME FROM THE <u>INSIDE</u>, NEVER THE OUTSIDE.

SOLVING A LOFTY PROBLEM

IF YOU CAN'T SEEM TO GET SUFFICIENT LOFT TO YOUR SHOTS, ESPECIALLY WITH THE DRIVER, CHANCES ARE YOU ARE COMMITTING ONE OR BOTH OF TWO ERRORS.

YOU MAY BE RIDING YOUR RIGHT SHOULDER TOO HIGH AS YOU HIT THROUGH, INSTEAD OF BRINGING IT DOWN AND UNDER THE BALL...

...OR YOU ARE MOVING YOUR HEAD BEYOND THE BALL. FOR PROPER LOFT, AS WELL AS CONTROL, THE HEAD MUST REMAIN *BEHIND* THE BALL AT ALL TIMES!

BARRETT TAYLOR

AVOIDING A PULL

THE HABIT OF CUTTING ACROSS THE BALL BY PULLING THE CLUBHEAD FROM AN OUTSIDE-TO-INSIDE PATH CAN GENERALLY BE ATTRIBUTED TO FAULTY WEIGHT SHIFT.

A LATE TRANSFER OF WEIGHT TO THE LEFT SIDE DURING THE DOWN-SWING WILL CAUSE THE UPPER PART OF THE BODY TO SWING OUT OVER THE TOP OF THE BALL...

WEIGHT INCORRECTLY ON RIGHT SIDE.

...AN ERROR YOU'LL FIND DIFFICULT TO COMMIT IF YOU CONCENTRATE ON GETTING YOUR WEIGHT QUICKLY ONTO YOUR LEFT FOOT WHILE BRINGING THE RIGHT SHOULDER DOWN UNDER THE BALL.

WEIGHT CORRECTLY ON LEFT SIDE.

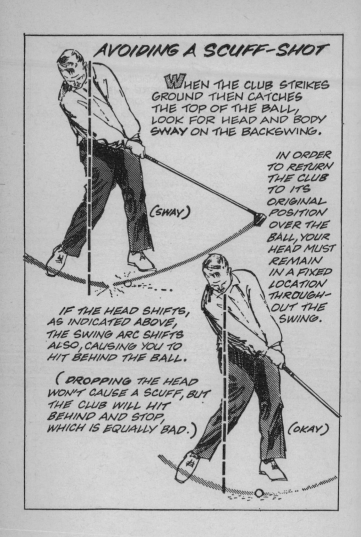

AVOIDING A SCUFF-SHOT

WHEN THE CLUB STRIKES GROUND THEN CATCHES THE TOP OF THE BALL, LOOK FOR HEAD AND BODY SWAY ON THE BACKSWING.

IN ORDER TO RETURN THE CLUB TO ITS ORIGINAL POSITION OVER THE BALL, YOUR HEAD MUST REMAIN IN A FIXED LOCATION THROUGHOUT THE SWING.

(SWAY)

IF THE HEAD SHIFTS, AS INDICATED ABOVE, THE SWING ARC SHIFTS ALSO, CAUSING YOU TO HIT BEHIND THE BALL.

(DROPPING THE HEAD WON'T CAUSE A SCUFF, BUT THE CLUB WILL HIT BEHIND AND STOP, WHICH IS EQUALLY BAD.)

(OKAY)

PART 1 • CURING THE DUCK HOOK

THE PLAGUING *DUCK-HOOK*, WHERE THE BALL TRAVELS 50 OR 100 YDS. THEN DIVES, HAS MANY CAUSES, BUT HERE STARTS A SERIES ON THE *FOUR* MAIN ONES.

FIRST, FAULTY RIGHT SHOULDER ACTION: THE BACKSWING CAN BE CORRECT BUT IF THE SHOULDER PULLS AROUND AS THE DOWNSWING BEGINS, THE ARC CHANGES...

INCORRECT: SHOULDER AROUND

...THE BODY TENDS TO WHIRL ON THE BALL, CREATING AN OUTSIDE-IN SWING PATH AND A CLOSED CLUBFACE AT IMPACT.

CORRECT: SHOULDER UNDER

PART II • CURING THE DUCK HOOK

A MAJOR CAUSE OF THE DUCK-HOOK IS TOO LITTLE WEIGHT SHIFT ON THE BACKSWING.

WHEN MOST OF THE WEIGHT REMAINS ON THE LEFT LEG, THE SWING IS CENTERED TOO FAR FORWARD. THE DOWNSWING WILL COME TOO MUCH FROM THE **INSIDE** AND FORCE A TENDENCY TO RELEASE THE CLUBHEAD TOO QUICKLY WITH EXCESS WRIST ROLL . . .

LINE OF TARGET

. . . A CLOSED FACE AND INSIDE-OUT SWING COMBINE TO CAUSE THE BALL TO HOOK AND DIVE. CORRECT BY GETTING WEIGHT ONTO YOUR **RIGHT** FOOT DURING THE BACKSWING!

PART III • CURING THE DUCK HOOK

ANOTHER CAUSE OF A DUCK-HOOK IS HITTING FROM A CLOSED CLUBFACE AT THE **TOP** OF THE SWING. THIS BEGINS BY TAKING THE CLUB **OUTSIDE** THE LINE OF DIRECTION ON THE TAKEAWAY, THEN CLOSING THE FACE BY PREMATURE WRIST BREAK.

TAKE THE CLUB **STRAIGHT** BACK, SETTING THE HANDS IN THE SAME RELATION YOU WANT THEM AT THE TOP.

IF CLUBFACE IS SQUARE AT TOP IT CAN RETURN TO THE BALL IN THE SAME POSITION.

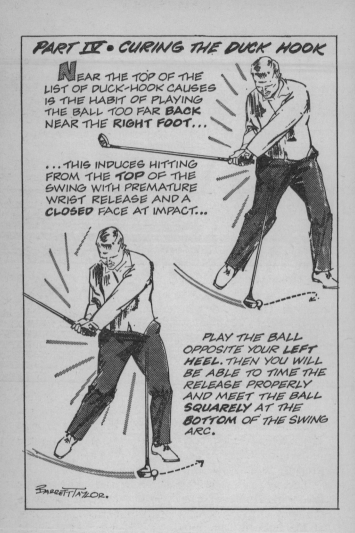

PART IV • CURING THE DUCK HOOK

NEAR THE TOP OF THE LIST OF DUCK-HOOK CAUSES IS THE HABIT OF PLAYING THE BALL TOO FAR **BACK** NEAR THE **RIGHT FOOT**...

...THIS INDUCES HITTING FROM THE **TOP** OF THE SWING WITH PREMATURE WRIST RELEASE AND A **CLOSED** FACE AT IMPACT...

PLAY THE BALL OPPOSITE YOUR **LEFT HEEL**. THEN YOU WILL BE ABLE TO TIME THE RELEASE PROPERLY AND MEET THE BALL **SQUARELY** AT THE **BOTTOM** OF THE SWING ARC.

BARRETT TAYLOR.

CHAPTER 5

Power and Accuracy

No matter how far some of us hit the ball, we're never absolutely satisfied. The man who consistently hits the ball 250 yards off the tee wants to reach 275 yards, while the longer hitter hungers to drive a ball 300 yards. The temptation to go for the long ball is a trait common to all golfers, and it's all right as long as you don't wind up sacrificing accuracy for distance.

In this chapter I have selected illustrated panels that will help to show you how to build up power without corrupting your swing. For the more we reach back for something extra, the more we increase our chances for error. Some small but integral part of the swing can be upset; the timing, the rhythm and the balance you have worked so hard at developing may come unwound like a two-dollar watch. Distance doesn't mean a thing if you can't keep your ball in play.

As most golfers do, I believe that power comes from the legs. They are the foundation of your swing and they transmit the sock that goes into your shot. If your legs don't work right, your whole swing will collapse.

So, let's cover some reminder-tips on the role of the legs. As your hips rotate to the right on the backswing, your left knee must move back gradually to a position *behind* the ball. A common fault among average golfers is that they let the knee fly straight out with their weight remaining on the ball of the left foot. But by concentrating on rolling the left foot from the inside, you will be able to bring the left knee back and keep the entire left side properly tucked in as the body coils.

The role of the right knee is both to steady and to power the swing. It must remain fixed to prevent any sway as the body turns away on the backswing, then push right at the hole through impact. By keeping your weight *inside* of the foot, your knee will remain stationary until the forward thrust occurs.

But never let power go to your head. It comes from your legs.

COILING for A FREE SWING

AS YOU REACH THE PEAK OF THE BACKSWING YOU SHOULD FEEL THAT YOUR RIGHT SIDE IS NEITHER LOCKED NOR LOOSELY RELAXED.

THE CORRECT FEELING IS ONE OF **COILED STRENGTH**— OF HAVING SOMETHING FROM WHICH TO **SPRING**.

THIS IS A SENSATION NOT OF TENSION BUT OF A CAPABILITY TO MOVE THE HIPS QUICKLY AND SMOOTHLY INTO THE DOWNSWING.

BARRETT TAYLOR

FAST HIPS ADD YARDAGE

WHENEVER I DESIRE A LITTLE EXTRA DISTANCE ON A DRIVE, I CONCENTRATE ON A FASTER HIP-TURN ON THE DOWNSWING; FOR THE FASTER THE HIPS TRAVEL FROM THE THE TOP OF THE SWING THROUGH IMPACT, THE GREATER THE CLUB SPEED GENERATED.

FASTER HIP-TURN CREATES GREATER LEVERAGE AND THUS MORE POWER IN THE DELAYED RELEASE.

...HOWEVER FAST YOU TURN YOUR HIPS, KEEP THE ACTION SMOOTH IN ORDER TO RETAIN TEMPO, RHYTHM AND BALANCE.

BARRETT TAYLOR

TIMING the HIP TURN

WHILE A FULL HIP TURN IS ESSENTIAL TO A FREE AND POWERFUL SWING, CARE MUST BE TAKEN NOT TO TURN THE HIPS TOO QUICKLY INTO THE BACKSWING.

THIS WILL CAUSE THE SHOULDER TURN TO BECOME TOO FLAT AND THEREBY CREATE AN OVERLY FLAT SWING PLANE. QUICK HIPS WILL ALSO CAUSE YOU TO "LAY OFF THE BALL". (BREAK WRISTS ON TAKEAWAY.)

FOR MAXIMUM EFFICIENCY AND COMPACTNESS OF SWING, KEEP EVERYTHING — HIPS SHOULDERS, ARMS — MOVING TOGETHER AT THE SAME GENERAL RATE OF SPEED.

BARRETT TAYLOR

HIT WITH BOTH HANDS

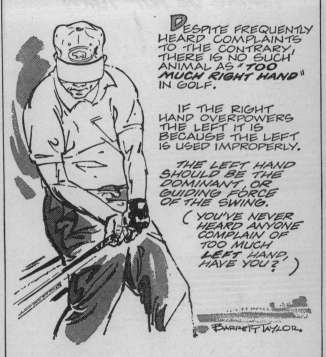

DESPITE FREQUENTLY HEARD COMPLAINTS TO THE CONTRARY, THERE IS NO SUCH ANIMAL AS *"TOO MUCH RIGHT HAND"* IN GOLF.

IF THE RIGHT HAND OVERPOWERS THE LEFT IT IS BECAUSE THE LEFT IS USED IMPROPERLY.

THE LEFT HAND SHOULD BE THE DOMINANT, OR GUIDING FORCE OF THE SWING.

(*YOU'VE NEVER HEARD ANYONE COMPLAIN OF TOO MUCH LEFT HAND, HAVE YOU?*)

BARRETT TAYLOR.

IF THE LEFT HAND IS LEADING AND FIRMLY IN CONTROL YOU CAN HIT AS HARD AS POSSIBLE WITH THE RIGHT HAND, AND YOU SHOULD. YOU HAVE TWO HANDS, SO USE THEM BOTH TO THE UTMOST.

BRACING FOR IMPACT

Just what is the **FIRM LEFT SIDE** experts tell you to hit against?

It is not a stiff, straight left leg at impact, as interpreted by many average players, for this stops hip-turn and throws the clubhead out over the top of the ball.

To create a firm left side against which to release maximum clubhead speed and control, the left leg must remain *slightly flexed* during the release and followthru, as at address. This allows hips to keep turning, brings the right shoulder down and keeps the club on line.

BARRETT TAYLOR

IMPACT CONTROL

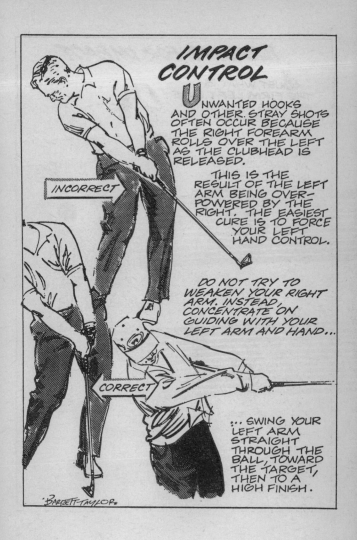

UNWANTED HOOKS AND OTHER STRAY SHOTS OFTEN OCCUR BECAUSE THE RIGHT FOREARM ROLLS OVER THE LEFT AS THE CLUBHEAD IS RELEASED.

THIS IS THE RESULT OF THE LEFT ARM BEING OVER-POWERED BY THE RIGHT. THE EASIEST CURE IS TO FORCE YOUR LEFT HAND CONTROL.

DO NOT TRY TO WEAKEN YOUR RIGHT ARM. INSTEAD, CONCENTRATE ON GUIDING WITH YOUR LEFT ARM AND HAND...

... SWING YOUR LEFT ARM STRAIGHT THROUGH THE BALL, TOWARD THE TARGET, THEN TO A HIGH FINISH.

INCORRECT

CORRECT

BARTLETT-TAYLOR

87

EXTEND YOURSELF!

IF IT'S CONTROL AND DIRECTION YOU ARE AFTER, KEEP YOUR FOLLOW-THROUGH *LOW*. EXTEND BOTH ARMS AS FAR AS POSSIBLE AFTER THE HIT WITH WEIGHT ON THE LEFT FOOT AND YOUR HEAD FIXED FIRMLY IN POSITION.

THIS GREATER EXTENSION ALLOWS YOU TO CATCH THE BALL AND SORT OF RIDE WITH IT; AND THE LONGER THE BALL REMAINS ON THE CLUBFACE, THE GREATER YOUR CHANCES OF HITTING IN THE DIRECTION OF THE HOLE.

AVOID!

AVOID PULLING UP QUICKLY AFTER THE HIT, AS THIS WILL CAUSE AN INCONSISTENT FLICKING ACTION.

LEFT ARM EXTENSION

TO ACHIEVE MAXIMUM EXTENSION THROUGH THE BALL, AND THEREBY PRODUCE STRAIGHTER SHOTS, THE *LEFT ARM* SHOULD REMAIN *STRAIGHT* FOR AS LONG AS POSSIBLE AFTER IMPACT— UNTIL THE RIGHT HAND FORCES IT TO BREAK NEAR THE FINISH.

THIS KEEPS THE CLUBFACE ON TARGET LONGER AND PREVENTS ANY CONTROL—ROBBING *CLIPPING* ACTION THAT RESULTS FROM THE LEFT ARM BREAKING TOO SOON AFTER THE HIT.

BEN HOGAN IS THE GREATEST EXAMPLE OF LEFT ARM EXTENSION. HIS ARM BREAKS ONLY SLIGHTLY AT THE VERY FINISH.

HIT THE AREA

To realize your full power potential, try to direct the climax of the club acceleration *THROUGH*, rather than *AT*, the ball.

You've often heard reference to the *"HITTING-ZONE"*...the area extending from several feet behind to several feet beyond the ball, through which the pent-up power of the hands is released...

BARRETT TAYLOR

...CONCENTRATING ON DELIVERING A SMOOTH FLOWING SWING THROUGH THIS AREA WILL PRODUCE ACCURACY AS WELL AS DISTANCE.

LET YOUR BODY FACE THE HOLE AT THE FINISH

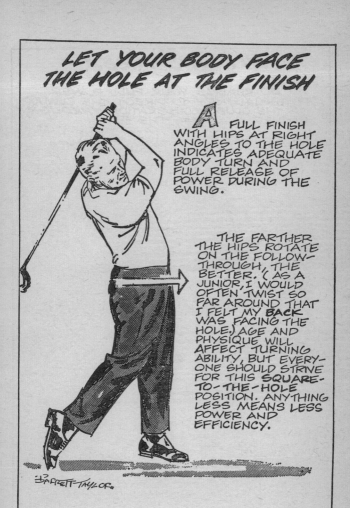

A FULL FINISH WITH HIPS AT RIGHT ANGLES TO THE HOLE INDICATES ADEQUATE BODY TURN AND FULL RELEASE OF POWER DURING THE SWING.

THE FARTHER THE HIPS ROTATE ON THE FOLLOW-THROUGH, THE BETTER. (AS A JUNIOR, I WOULD OFTEN TWIST SO FAR AROUND THAT I FELT MY **BACK** WAS FACING THE HOLE.) AGE AND PHYSIQUE WILL AFFECT TURNING ABILITY, BUT EVERY-ONE SHOULD STRIVE FOR THIS **SQUARE-TO-THE-HOLE** POSITION. ANYTHING LESS MEANS LESS POWER AND EFFICIENCY.

BARRETT TAYLOR.

WHAT YOUR FINISHING GRIP WILL TELL YOU

THE BEST WAY TO TELL IF YOUR GRIP HAS BEEN FIRM AT IMPACT IS TO CHECK IT AT THE **FINISH** OF YOUR SWING.

ENDING WITH A LOOSE HOLD ON THE CLUB SHOWS YOU'VE BECOME SLOPPY AND FIRMNESS HAS BEEN LOST SOMEWHERE ALONG THE LINE—ON THE TAKEAWAY, NEAR THE TOP OF THE BACK-SWING OR AT THE BEGINNING OF THE DOWNSWING. AS A RESULT, YOUR GRIP VARIES FROM SWING TO SWING, AND SO DOES THE FLIGHT OF THE BALL.

FOR CONSISTENT POWER AND CONTROL AT IMPACT, YOUR GRIP MUST REMAIN FIRM AND UNCHANGED AT ALL TIMES.

COIL for POWER

To generate maximum power in the golf swing, a full coiling of the body on the backswing is essential.

With the driver, I feel that I am coiling my legs, hips, arms and shoulders just about as far around as they will go.

This is phase one in creating a large swing arc and building power for release at the ball. Next I will discuss phase two, which is a part of coiling.

BARRETT TAYLOR

CHAPTER 6

Recovering from Sand

To the duffer who finds his ball in a sand bunker, any way he can get it out and headed toward safe ground is the best way to get out. But to the experienced player who's been there before, getting the ball out of the bunker and into the cup in the shortest possible number of strokes is the best way. There are tried-and-true methods for accomplishing this, and that's what this chapter is all about.

The problems I will deal with in this section are aimed at the advanced golfer who's looking for more than simply a way of recovering from sand. These tips have to do with such testing situations as playing from buried lies, having to make the ball rise quickly to avoid an overhanging lip, and imparting backspin so that your ball will hold a green—where finessing your way out of a bunker is just as important as blasting your way out.

We start, of course, with the premise that you already know the way to come out of sand under conventional circumstances. But since everything we do in golf is predicated on the basics, let's just review some of the procedures you should have learned in your first lesson in bunker play. The primary rule in bunker shots is to take sand behind the ball, not to hit the ball cleanly. In addressing your ball, make sure your feet are firmly planted in the sand and hit from an open stance. On short-range bunker shots, you cock your wrists earlier than usual, and you always cut across the ball in an outside-in arc.

Bunker play may be a terrible trial to you, but you can win the verdict every time by having a positive attitude.

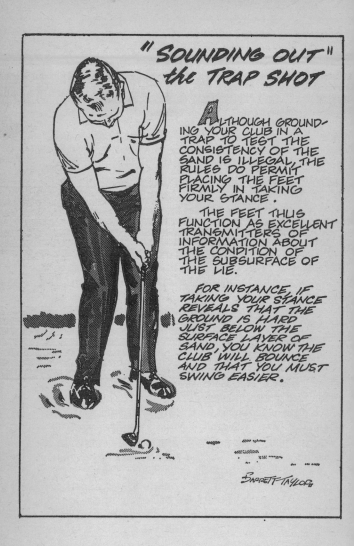

"SOUNDING OUT" the TRAP SHOT

ALTHOUGH GROUNDING YOUR CLUB IN A TRAP TO TEST THE CONSISTENCY OF THE SAND IS ILLEGAL, THE RULES DO PERMIT PLACING THE FEET FIRMLY IN TAKING YOUR STANCE.

THE FEET THUS FUNCTION AS EXCELLENT TRANSMITTERS OF INFORMATION ABOUT THE CONDITION OF THE SUBSURFACE OF THE LIE.

FOR INSTANCE, IF TAKING YOUR STANCE REVEALS THAT THE GROUND IS HARD JUST BELOW THE SURFACE LAYER OF SAND, YOU KNOW THE CLUB WILL BOUNCE AND THAT YOU MUST SWING EASIER.

BARRETT-TAYLOR

PLAYING the 4 WOOD from A TRAP

ALTHOUGH MANY EXPERTS ADVISE AGAINST USING A WOOD FROM A FAIRWAY BUNKER, I FIND THAT IN CERTAIN CIRCUMSTANCES, THE *FOUR WOOD* (OR 3 WOOD) CAN PRODUCE BETTER RESULTS THAN ANY IRON.

IF I AM IN A TRAP 175 YDS. FROM THE GREEN, I WILL NORMALLY USE A 5 IRON—BUT IF TOO MUCH SAND PREVENTS ME FROM GETTING TO THE BALL FIRST AND HITTING CLEANLY, I'LL TAKE THE 4 WOOD AND HIT A *CUT BLAST* SHOT.

THE HANDS ARE TURNED TO THE LEFT IN A FADE POSITION AND THE BODY IS ALIGNED TO THE LEFT OF THE TARGET.

AS I HIT JUST IN BACK OF THE BALL, THE HEAVY ROUNDED HEAD OF THE 4 WOOD WILL DIG THROUGH THE SAND AND THE BALL WILL FLY OUT WITH A SURPRISING AMOUNT OF LOFT AND DISTANCE. SINCE THE SAND PREVENTS SOLID CONTACT WITH THE BALL, THERE IS LITTLE DANGER OF OVER-SHOOTING THE GREEN.

WHEREAS AN IRON MAY PRODUCE ONLY 90 YDS. OF DISTANCE FROM THIS LIE, A 4 WOOD MAY ENABLE YOU TO REACH THE GREEN OR, AT LEAST, SHORTEN THE NEXT SHOT.

B. TAYLOR

97

AVOID EXTREMES in CHOOSING A SAND WEDGE

CONTRARY TO POPULAR BELIEF, THE IDEAL SAND WEDGE DOES NOT POSSESS AN EXTREMELY WIDE FLANGE. GRANTED, THIS TYPE WORKS BEST FOR PERFECT LIES, BUT FOR THE VARIETY OF LIES ENCOUNTERED IN TRAP PLAY THE WEDGE WITH A *"MEDIUM"* FLANGE OFFERS THE BEST OVERALL PERFORMANCE.

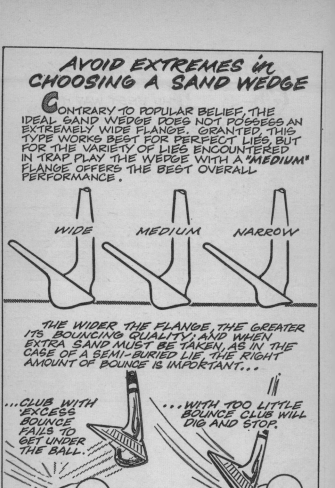

WIDE   MEDIUM   NARROW

THE WIDER THE FLANGE, THE GREATER ITS BOUNCING QUALITY; AND WHEN EXTRA SAND MUST BE TAKEN, AS IN THE CASE OF A SEMI-BURIED LIE, THE RIGHT AMOUNT OF BOUNCE IS IMPORTANT...

...CLUB WITH EXCESS BOUNCE FAILS TO GET UNDER THE BALL.

...WITH TOO LITTLE BOUNCE CLUB WILL DIG AND STOP.

BARRETT TAYLOR

PRACTICING SAND SHOTS

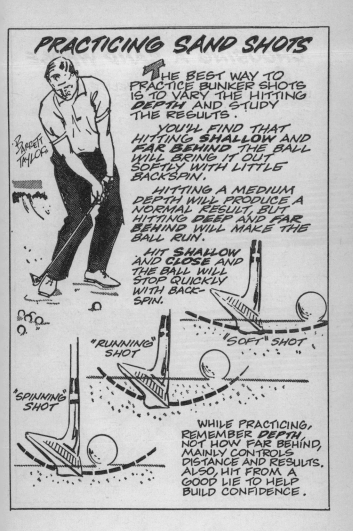

THE BEST WAY TO PRACTICE BUNKER SHOTS IS TO VARY THE HITTING *DEPTH* AND STUDY THE RESULTS.

YOU'LL FIND THAT HITTING **SHALLOW** AND **FAR BEHIND** THE BALL WILL BRING IT OUT SOFTLY WITH LITTLE BACKSPIN.

HITTING A MEDIUM DEPTH WILL PRODUCE A NORMAL RESULT, BUT HITTING **DEEP** AND **FAR BEHIND** WILL MAKE THE BALL RUN.

HIT **SHALLOW** AND **CLOSE** AND THE BALL WILL STOP QUICKLY WITH BACK-SPIN.

"SOFT" SHOT

"RUNNING" SHOT

"SPINNING" SHOT

WHILE PRACTICING, REMEMBER *DEPTH*, NOT HOW FAR BEHIND, MAINLY CONTROLS DISTANCE AND RESULTS. ALSO, HIT FROM A GOOD LIE TO HELP BUILD CONFIDENCE.

PUTTING BRAKES on a BLAST

IN TRAP PLAY THE SYSTEM USED TO IMPART BACKSPIN AND STOP A BALL QUICKLY INVOLVES, MAINLY, TWO DEPARTURES FROM NORMAL.

FIRST, THE CLUBHEAD MUST ENTER THE SAND ONLY **ONE** INCH BEHIND THE BALL INSTEAD OF THE CUSTOMARY TWO. THE PRINCIPLE BEING, THE **LESS** SAND GETTING BETWEEN THE CLUBFACE AND BALL THE **GREATER** THE BACKSPIN.

HITTING CLOSE TO THE BALL WILL SEND IT FARTHER THAN NORMAL. COMPENSATE BY HITTING DEEPER INTO THE SAND.

NORMAL SHOT

STOPPING SHOT

HIT BOTH CLOSER AND DEEPER USING A NORMAL STRENGTH SWING.

BARRETT TAYLOR

MAKING THE BALL RISE

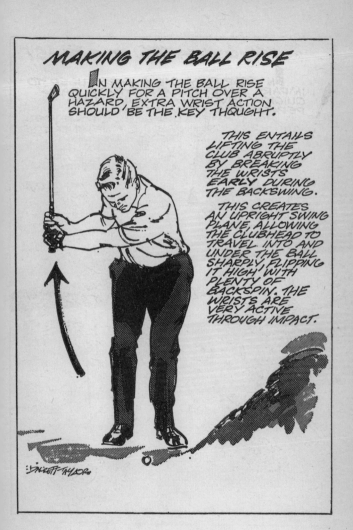

IN MAKING THE BALL RISE QUICKLY FOR A PITCH OVER A HAZARD, EXTRA WRIST ACTION SHOULD BE THE KEY THOUGHT.

THIS ENTAILS LIFTING THE CLUB ABRUPTLY BY BREAKING THE WRISTS EARLY DURING THE BACKSWING.

THIS CREATES AN UPRIGHT SWING PLANE, ALLOWING THE CLUBHEAD TO TRAVEL INTO AND UNDER THE BALL SHARPLY, FLIPPING IT HIGH WITH PLENTY OF BACKSPIN. THE WRISTS ARE VERY ACTIVE THROUGH IMPACT.

The RUNNING TRAP SHOT

AS MENTIONED LAST, THE **CLOSER** YOU HIT TO A BALL IN SAND, THE **GREATER** THE BACKSPIN POSSIBLE. SO, IT IS REASONABLE AND QUITE CORRECT TO ASSUME THAT IN ORDER TO **LESSEN** BACKSPIN AND RUN THE BALL THE CLUBHEAD MUST ENTER THE SAND **FARTHER** FROM THE BALL.

HIT 2½ OR 3 INCHES BEHIND THE BALL INSTEAD OF THE NORMAL 2 INCHES. IN ADDITION, DO NOT GO AS DEEPLY AS USUAL. SINCE THE CLUBHEAD WILL HAVE FARTHER TO TRAVEL THROUGH THE SAND, A SHALLOW HIT WILL CUT RESISTANCE AND PREVENT DUMPING THE SHOT.

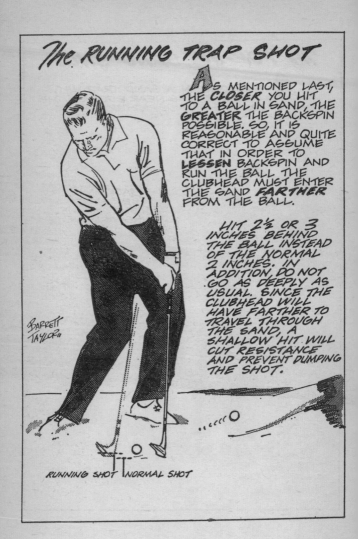

BARRETT TAYLOR"

RUNNING SHOT   NORMAL SHOT

The "POP-UP" SAND SHOT

A BURIED LIE IN A SAND TRAP WITH THE PIN CLOSE TO THE NEAR EDGE OF THE GREEN CALLS FOR A DEPARTURE FROM ORDINARY BURIED LIE METHODS IN ORDER TO MAKE THE BALL RISE QUICKLY.

OPEN THE CLUBFACE WIDE THEN BREAK THE WRISTS EARLY ON THE BACKSWING...

...THIS PRODUCES AN UPRIGHT PLANE ON THE BACKSWING AND A STEEP ANGLE OF DESCENT ON THE DOWNSWING. SINCE AN OPEN FACE TENDS TO BOUNCE OFF SAND THE RIGHT HAND MUST DOMINATE THE HITTING ACTION IN ORDER TO DRIVE THE CLUB-HEAD BENEATH THE BALL. HIT AS CLOSE TO THE BALL AS POSSIBLE WHILE MAKING SURE TO GET UNDER IT.

THE BALL SHOULD "POP" OUT WITH PLENTY OF BACKSPIN.

BARRETT TAYLOR

BALL POSITIONING for SAND

THOUGH BALL POSITION WILL VARY WITH DIFFERENT SITUATIONS, YOU'LL FIND A LOCATION OPPOSITE THE LEFT *INSTEP* BEST FOR AVERAGE SAND SHOTS.

FAIRWAY

BUNKER

WHILE NORMAL FAIRWAY SHOTS ARE PLAYED WITH THE BALL OPPOSITE THE LEFT HEEL, HERE YOU ARE HITTING, NOT THE BALL, BUT **SAND**, ABOUT 2 INCHES **BEHIND** IT. THEREFORE, YOU MUST COMPENSATE ACCORDINGLY SO THE CLUB REACHES THE PROPER POINT OF IMPACT AT THE BOTTOM OF THE SWING'S ARC.

BARRETT TAYLOR

CONSIDER SLOPE BEFORE BLASTING

READING THE GREEN SHOULD BE A STRONG RULE FOR SAND PLAY AS WELL AS FOR PUTTING. BUT SINCE YOU ARE HITTING WITH A **CUTTING**, OR SLICING ACTION THAT PLACES A **CLOCK-WISE SPIN** ON THE BALL, SLOPE EFFECT WILL VARY FROM NORMAL.

ON A **LEFT-TO-RIGHT** BREAK, SPIN WILL CAUSE THE BALL TO BREAK **MORE** THAN IS NORMAL...

...WHILE THE BALL WILL BREAK **LESS** THAN USUAL ON A **RIGHT-TO-LEFT** SLOPE.

DIG IN for LONG BLAST

IN PLAYING A *FULL LONG IRON* FROM A FAIRWAY TRAP, FIRST NOTE LOFT REQUIRED TO CARRY THE FRONT LIP. IF THE WAY IS CLEAR AND DISTANCE CALLS FOR A 3 IRON, TAKE A 2 IRON AND *CHOKE IT DOWN*. THIS PROVIDES BETTER CONTROL AND COMPENSATES FOR THE FACT THAT STANDING IN SAND PLACES YOU CLOSER TO THE BALL.

PLANT FEET FIRMLY — ESPECIALLY THE RIGHT — THEN TAKE A FULL PRACTICE SWING TO MAKE SURE YOU WON'T SLIP.

USE AN *UPRIGHT* BACKSWING AND, TO INSURE SOLID CONTACT, AIM AT THE *TOP* OF THE BALL, NOT THE BACK.

The BOLD WAY OUT

When a nasty bunker lie, like the one pictured, makes you feel like calling it a day— DON'T! Properly executed, such a shot might provide a psychological boost toward a good score.

TRY THIS: Take as steady a stance as possible, choke up the club and open its face wide. To get the club past the lip, pick it up sharply. Also, take it to the outside of the line to the ball...

The downswing must be outside-in to produce a cutting action and raise the ball quickly. Be sure to strike the ball firmly with the right hand.

BARRETT TAYLOR

WHEN THE BALL LIES LOWER THAN THE FEET

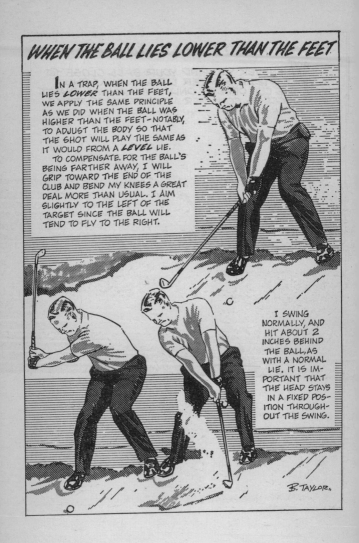

IN A TRAP, WHEN THE BALL LIES *LOWER* THAN THE FEET, WE APPLY THE SAME PRINCIPLE AS WE DID WHEN THE BALL WAS HIGHER THAN THE FEET—NOTABLY, TO ADJUST THE BODY SO THAT THE SHOT WILL PLAY THE SAME AS IT WOULD FROM A *LEVEL* LIE.

TO COMPENSATE FOR THE BALL'S BEING FARTHER AWAY, I WILL GRIP TOWARD THE END OF THE CLUB AND BEND MY KNEES A GREAT DEAL MORE THAN USUAL. I AIM SLIGHTLY TO THE LEFT OF THE TARGET SINCE THE BALL WILL TEND TO FLY TO THE RIGHT.

I SWING NORMALLY, AND HIT ABOUT 2 INCHES BEHIND THE BALL, AS WITH A NORMAL LIE. IT IS IMPORTANT THAT THE HEAD STAYS IN A FIXED POSITION THROUGHOUT THE SWING.

B. TAYLOR.

LONG ROUTE MAY BE BEST

WHENEVER YOU FIND YOUR BALL CLOSE TO A VERY STEEP BUNKER LIP AND BLASTING FOR THE CUP OFFERS ONLY A MARGINAL CHANCE FOR SUCCESS, CONSIDER AN *ALTERNATE* ROUTE.

YOU MAY FIND IT POSSIBLE TO AVOID THE BLOCKADE BY DIRECTING THE SHOT, SAY, 20 FEET RIGHT OR LEFT OF THE HOLE. THE CARDINAL RULE FOR PLAYING SAND IS *FIRST, GET THE BALL OUT!* LEAVING A LONGER PUTT BEATS WASTING STROKES IN A "MIRACLE SHOT" ATTEMPT. SO PLAY THE POSITIVE ROUTE, THEN TAKE IT FROM THERE.

BARRETT TAYLOR

CHAPTER 7

Putting to Win

From tee to green, most golf professionals are fairly even. We all hit the ball about the same distance, give or take a few yards, and we all have the shots to get us onto the putting surface in regulation figures. But it is probably on the greens themselves that most tournaments are won and lost. Putting is the great equalizer.

The basic law of the greens is that you must putt with a purpose. Simply slapping the ball with the blade of your putter without having a plan in mind is like playing pin the tail on the donkey blindfolded. The illustrations I've prepared for this section should show you that good putting is an acquired art, not an inborn one.

But while the winning and losing of a round is often decided on the greens, the strategy-minded golfer can make his move even before he gets there. Sometimes, you can help your putting by planning an intelligent approach shot. For example, in judging approach distances, it is important to remember that greens can be several clubs in depth. If you are standing approximately 100 yards from the front edge of a green some 75 yards in length, you can use any of a number of short-irons in your bag. It all depends on the pin placement. If the pin is in front, you may use your wedge and stop it up close to the pin. But if it's deeper back on the putting surface, that same wedge will leave you a couple of putts from the cup. In this case, perhaps a five- or a seven-iron should be used to get you closer to the hole. That's one way of saving actual putts.

And when you get a chance to practice putts, don't just go for the 40- and 50-footers. How many of those does anybody really expect to sink? Practice long putts for lagging purposes only—develop a consistent style and you'll sink your share of those. But confidence and accuracy are acquired from 12 feet in. Putts of this length you should expect to make frequently. Don't forget those four-footers, either. Learn to sink them and you won't be afraid of those long ones that fail to die right at the hole.

PUTTING the SHORT SLIDER

IN ORDER TO HOLD THE LINE ON BREAKING PUTTS OF 3 FEET OR LESS, USE A *FIRM*, BOLD STROKE.

MANY PLAYERS MISTAKENLY TRY TO "DIE" THE BALL INTO THE HOLE WITH A GENTLE, DELICATE STROKE, AN APPROACH REFERRED TO AS "PLAYING THE BALL OUT OF THE HOLE." IT REQUIRES THAT BOTH SPEED *AND* DIRECTION BE PERFECT. THE FIRM METHOD REQUIRES PERFECT DIRECTION ONLY, SO YOU ELIMINATE ONE FACTOR.

EASY *FIRM*

BARRETT TAYLOR

YOU'LL FIND THE FASTER-TRAVELING BALL WILL NOT BREAK AS SHARPLY AND, IN MOST CASES, NEEDS LITTLE, IF ANY, BORROW TO DROP.

CHECK for SQUARENESS

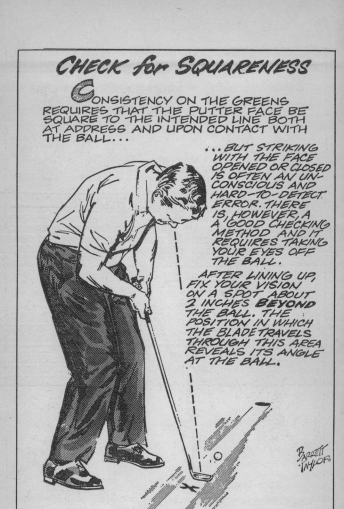

CONSISTENCY ON THE GREENS REQUIRES THAT THE PUTTER FACE BE SQUARE TO THE INTENDED LINE BOTH AT ADDRESS AND UPON CONTACT WITH THE BALL...

...BUT STRIKING WITH THE FACE OPENED OR CLOSED IS OFTEN AN UN-CONSCIOUS AND HARD-TO-DETECT ERROR. THERE IS, HOWEVER, A 'GOOD CHECKING METHOD AND IT REQUIRES TAKING YOUR EYES OFF THE BALL.

AFTER LINING UP, FIX YOUR VISION ON A SPOT ABOUT 2 INCHES **BEYOND** THE BALL. THE POSITION IN WHICH THE BLADE TRAVELS THROUGH THIS AREA REVEALS ITS ANGLE AT THE BALL.

BARRETT TAYLOR

FOR SOLID PUTTS KEEP YOUR FINISH LOW

THE PURPOSE OF A LOW FOLLOW-THROUGH IN PUTTING IS TO KEEP THE BLADE FROM COMING UP AND APPLYING EXCESS OVERSPIN TO THE BALL.

ALTHOUGH I PURPOSELY RAISE MY FINISH TO GET MORE ROLLING ACTION ON SOME SHORT PUTTS, FOR THE MAJORITY OF CASES, I FIND A LOW FINISH HELPS TO ATTAIN A MORE SOLID AND CON-SISTENT STROKE.

STRAIGHT FACE is BEST

PICTURED ARE **3** POSITIONS IN WHICH THE PUTTER FACE CAN ADDRESS AND STRIKE THE BALL. ALL ARE USED BY GOOD PLAYERS, BUT I CONSIDER NO. **3** MOST IDEAL.

BLADE LAID BACK WITH HANDS BEHIND— CREATES MORE OVERSPIN FOR EASE OF RUN, BUT CAUSES AN INCONSISTENCY IN DISTANCE BECAUSE OF A TENDENCY TO TOP THE BALL SOMEWHAT AT TIMES.	BLADE SLIGHTLY HOODED WITH HANDS FORWARD— PROVIDES SOLID CONTACT BY VIRTUE OF DOWNWARD BLOW, BUT SINCE BALL IS DRIVEN INTO THE SURFACE IT MAY REACT ERRATICALLY ON SOME GREENS.	HANDS IN LINE WITH VERTICALLY STRAIGHT SHAFT AND BLADE— PRODUCES THE MOST **CONSISTENT** ROLL OF THE THREE. TRY EACH STYLE AND STUDY THE RESULTS.

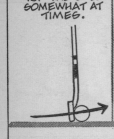 

SHORT PUTT TROUBLES? LET PUTTER SWING ITSELF

IF YOU ARE HAVING TROUBLE WITH SHORT PUTTS OF 3 OR 4 FEET, HERE IS A SYSTEM THAT MAY HELP YOU JUST AS IT HAS HELPED ME ON NUMEROUS OCCASIONS.

SIMPLY TAKE THE PUTTER BACK TWICE AS FAR AS YOU HAVE BEEN AND HIT A LITTLE EASIER. THIS LETS THE PUTTER, RATHER THAN YOURSELF, DO THE WORK THUS SMOOTHING OUT THE STROKE AND RE-ESTABLISHING CONTROL.

BARRETT-TAYLOR

PUTTING from THE FRINGE

THE DECISION OF WHETHER TO **CHIP** OR **PUTT** FROM THE FRINGE OF THE GREEN DEPENDS PRIMARILY ON WHICH YOU HAVE THE MOST CONFIDENCE IN — YOUR CHIPS OR YOUR PUTTS.

IN MOST CASES I WOULD RECOMMEND THE PUTTER. YOU PUTT SO MANY MORE SHOTS THAN YOU CHIP, YOU'RE BOUND TO BE BETTER WITH THE PUTTER.

PERSONALLY, I MAY PUTT FROM TEN FEET OFF THE GREEN — I HAVE PUTTED FROM 30 YDS., WHEN THAT WAS THE ONLY SHOT LEFT. ON THE OTHER HAND, I'VE CHIPPED FROM ONLY 6 INCHES OFF THE GREEN, SINCE THE CONDITION OF THE SURFACE THAT THE BALL MUST COME OFF OF OFTEN DICTATES THE CHOICE OF CLUB.

IF THE GRASS IS RELATIVELY SMOOTH AND THE GRAIN RUNS TOWARD THE HOLE, SO THERE IS NO DANGER OF POPPING THE BALL UP INTO THE AIR, THEN THE PUTTER IS FINE.

WITH THE GRAIN AGAINST YOU, THE BALL MUST BE STROKED HARDER WITH THE PUTTER AND WILL COME OFF THE FRINGE VERY FAST. IT WOULD BE BETTER TO **PITCH** THE BALL ONTO THE GREEN AND LET IT DRIBBLE UP TO THE HOLE, ESPECIALLY IF THE HOLE IS CLOSE.

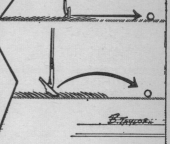

HANDLING DOWNHILL BREAKS

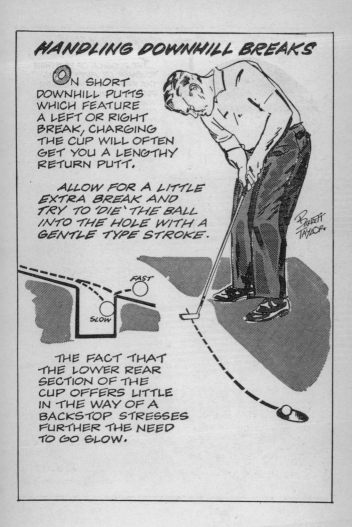

ON SHORT DOWNHILL PUTTS WHICH FEATURE A LEFT OR RIGHT BREAK, CHARGING THE CUP WILL OFTEN GET YOU A LENGTHY RETURN PUTT.

ALLOW FOR A LITTLE EXTRA BREAK AND TRY TO 'DIE' THE BALL INTO THE HOLE WITH A GENTLE TYPE STROKE.

FAST

SLOW

THE FACT THAT THE LOWER REAR SECTION OF THE CUP OFFERS LITTLE IN THE WAY OF A BACKSTOP STRESSES FURTHER THE NEED TO GO SLOW.

BACKSWING IS DISTANCE GAUGE

IN MEETING DISTANCE REQUIREMENTS FOR PUTTS, LENGTH OF BACKSWING RATHER THAN STRIKING FORCE SHOULD BE THE CONTROLLING FACTOR. BASICALLY, THIS MEANS THE LONGER THE PUTT, THE LONGER THE BACKSTROKE.

THOUGH THE LENGTH OF THE BACKSWING WILL VARY, I FEEL THAT THE PUTTER SHOULD SORT OF SWING ITSELF, AND TRAVEL AT THE SAME GENERAL RATE OF SPEED ON ALL PUTTS.

AS PUTTS LENGTHEN THERE IS A SLIGHT PROPORTIONAL INCREASE IN THE APPLIED HITTING STRENGTH. GENERALLY, HOWEVER, YOU SHOULD LET THE PUTTER SWING FREELY BY TAKING AN ADEQUATE BACKSWING. IT'S PRETTY HARD TO **FORCE** THE PUTTER IN ANY CERTAIN DIRECTION WITHOUT UPSETTING PRECISION.

PUTTING DOWNHILL

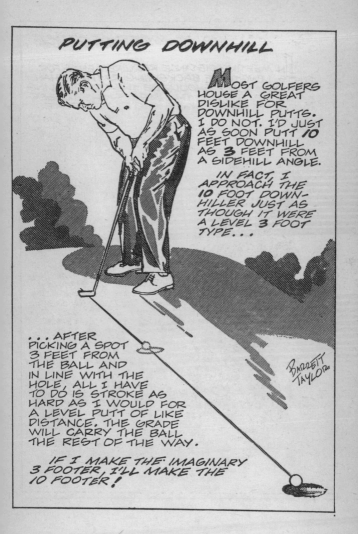

MOST GOLFERS HOUSE A GREAT DISLIKE FOR DOWNHILL PUTTS. I DO NOT. I'D JUST AS SOON PUTT *10* FEET DOWNHILL AS *3* FEET FROM A SIDEHILL ANGLE.

IN FACT I APPROACH THE 10 FOOT DOWN-HILLER JUST AS THOUGH IT WERE A LEVEL *3* FOOT TYPE...

... AFTER PICKING A SPOT 3 FEET FROM THE BALL AND IN LINE WITH THE HOLE, ALL I HAVE TO DO IS STROKE AS HARD AS I WOULD FOR A LEVEL PUTT OF LIKE DISTANCE. THE GRADE WILL CARRY THE BALL THE REST OF THE WAY.

IF I MAKE THE IMAGINARY 3 FOOTER, I'LL MAKE THE 10 FOOTER!

BARRETT TAYLOR

PUTTING WET GREENS

BASICALLY, THERE ARE *TWO* TYPES OF WET GREENS. ONE TYPE DEVELOPS IN EARLY SPRING WHEN THE MOISTURE GOES ALL THE WAY THROUGH THE GRASS AND INTO THE GROUND.

THIS SLOWS THE PUTT CONSIDERABLY AND REQUIRES A **FIRM** STROKE. THE FACT THAT THE BALL WILL NOT BREAK AS MUCH AS UNDER NORMAL CONDITIONS ENABLES YOU TO PUTT MORE BOLDLY AT THE HOLE.

THE OTHER TYPE OCCURS LATER WHEN THE COURSE IS FIRM — AFTER A SHORT RAIN THAT WETS SURFACE ONLY.

WATCH OUT FOR THIS TYPE! THE GREENS AREN'T REALLY WET UNDERNEATH, THOUGH THEY APPEAR TO BE. THIS SURFACE FILM WILL NOT AFFECT THE PUTT SIGNIFICANTLY — ONLY A TRIFLE.

BARRETT TAYLOR

FORWARD PRESS in PUTTING

THE USE OF A FORWARD PRESS IN PUTTING IS OPTIONAL, BUT IF YOU HAVE TROUBLE IN TAKING THE PUTTER AWAY SMOOTHLY ON THE BACKSWING, I SUGGEST YOU TRY IT.

WHEREAS THE FORWARD PRESS USED FOR TEE AND FAIRWAY SHOTS IS A COMBINATION HAND AND BODY MOTION, FOR PUTTING, ONLY THE WRISTS BEND SLIGHTLY TOWARD THE HOLE. THE BACKSWING IS THEN A SLOW RECOIL FROM THIS ACTION.

THE FORWARD PRESS DOES HAVE A TENDENCY TO OPEN THE PUTTER FACE SLIGHTLY. LESSEN THIS TENDENCY BY KEEPING THE FORWARD ACTION TO A MINIMUM.

BARRETT TAYLOR.

READING the GREEN

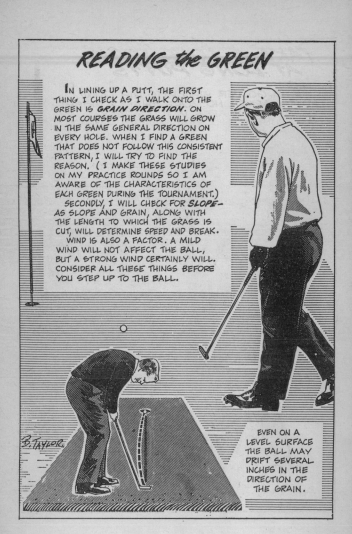

IN LINING UP A PUTT, THE FIRST THING I CHECK AS I WALK ONTO THE GREEN IS *GRAIN DIRECTION*. ON MOST COURSES THE GRASS WILL GROW IN THE SAME GENERAL DIRECTION ON EVERY HOLE. WHEN I FIND A GREEN THAT DOES NOT FOLLOW THIS CONSISTENT PATTERN, I WILL TRY TO FIND THE REASON. (I MAKE THESE STUDIES ON MY PRACTICE ROUNDS SO I AM AWARE OF THE CHARACTERISTICS OF EACH GREEN DURING THE TOURNAMENT.)

SECONDLY, I WILL CHECK FOR *SLOPE*- AS SLOPE AND GRAIN, ALONG WITH THE LENGTH TO WHICH THE GRASS IS CUT, WILL DETERMINE SPEED AND BREAK.

WIND IS ALSO A FACTOR. A MILD WIND WILL NOT AFFECT THE BALL, BUT A STRONG WIND CERTAINLY WILL. CONSIDER ALL THESE THINGS BEFORE YOU STEP UP TO THE BALL.

B. TAYLOR

EVEN ON A LEVEL SURFACE THE BALL MAY DRIFT SEVERAL INCHES IN THE DIRECTION OF THE GRAIN.

TAKE A LONG LOOK AT LONG PUTTS

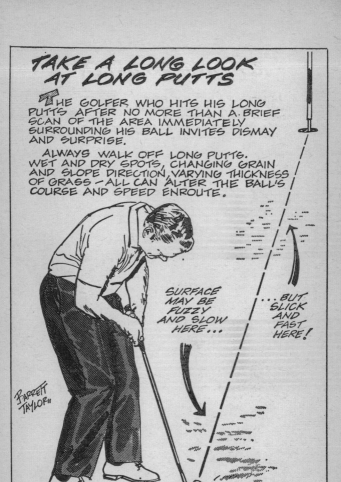

THE GOLFER WHO HITS HIS LONG PUTTS AFTER NO MORE THAN A BRIEF SCAN OF THE AREA IMMEDIATELY SURROUNDING HIS BALL INVITES DISMAY AND SURPRISE.

ALWAYS WALK OFF LONG PUTTS. WET AND DRY SPOTS, CHANGING GRAIN AND SLOPE DIRECTION, VARYING THICKNESS OF GRASS — ALL CAN ALTER THE BALL'S COURSE AND SPEED ENROUTE.

SURFACE MAY BE FUZZY AND SLOW HERE...

...BUT SLICK AND FAST HERE!

BARRETT TAYLOR

A RULE TO REMEMBER

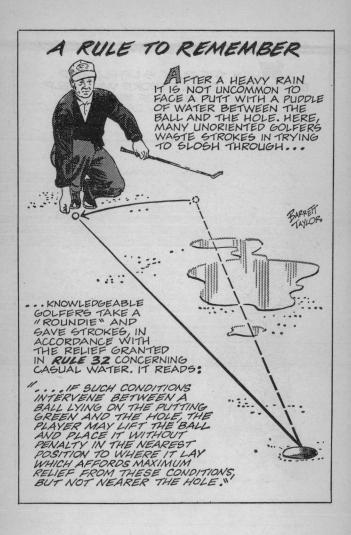

AFTER A HEAVY RAIN IT IS NOT UNCOMMON TO FACE A PUTT WITH A PUDDLE OF WATER BETWEEN THE BALL AND THE HOLE. HERE, MANY UNORIENTED GOLFERS WASTE STROKES IN TRYING TO SLOSH THROUGH...

BARRETT TAYLOR

...KNOWLEDGEABLE GOLFERS TAKE A "ROUNDIE" AND SAVE STROKES, IN ACCORDANCE WITH THE RELIEF GRANTED IN **RULE 32** CONCERNING CASUAL WATER. IT READS:

"....IF SUCH CONDITIONS INTERVENE BETWEEN A BALL LYING ON THE PUTTING GREEN AND THE HOLE, THE PLAYER MAY LIFT THE BALL AND PLACE IT WITHOUT PENALTY IN THE NEAREST POSITION TO WHERE IT LAY WHICH AFFORDS MAXIMUM RELIEF FROM THESE CONDITIONS, BUT NOT NEARER THE HOLE."

124

HANDLING THE UPHILL BREAK

WHEN THE PUTT IS UPHILL AND BREAKING, A **FIRM** STROKE WILL HELP REDUCE THE AMOUNT OF BREAK AS WELL AS ASSURE YOU REACH THE HOLE.

TAKE A **3** FOOTER WITH A SLIGHT BREAK FROM RIGHT TO LEFT. AIM FOR THE RIGHT CORNER OF THE CUP AND STROKE FIRMLY TO HOLD THE LINE.

UPHILL, THERE IS LITTLE DANGER OF RUNNING FAR PAST, AND THE HIGH REAR EDGE OF THE CUP SERVES AS A BACKSTOP. SO DON'T LEAVE 'EM SHORT*!*

BARRETT TAYLOR

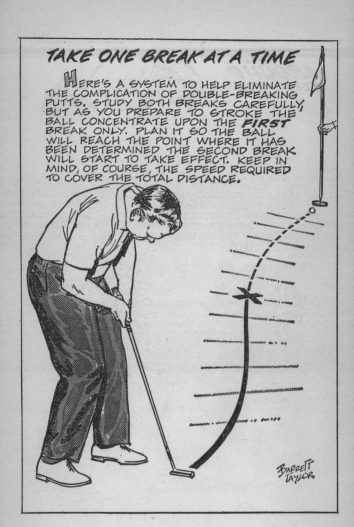

TAKE ONE BREAK AT A TIME

HERE'S A SYSTEM TO HELP ELIMINATE THE COMPLICATION OF DOUBLE-BREAKING PUTTS. STUDY BOTH BREAKS CAREFULLY, BUT AS YOU PREPARE TO STROKE THE BALL CONCENTRATE UPON THE *FIRST* BREAK ONLY. PLAN IT SO THE BALL WILL REACH THE POINT WHERE IT HAS BEEN DETERMINED THE SECOND BREAK WILL START TO TAKE EFFECT. KEEP IN MIND, OF COURSE, THE SPEED REQUIRED TO COVER THE TOTAL DISTANCE.

CHECK AROUND THE CUP

SINCE A DYING BALL IS AFFECTED MOST BY SURFACE IRREGULARITIES, A SPECIAL SURVEY OF THE AREA NEAR THE HOLE SHOULD BE AN IMPORTANT PART OF PRE-PUTT PLANNING.

THIS IS ESPECIALLY CRITICAL IN PERIODS OF SLOW GROWTH, WHEN GRASS CANNOT RECOVER EASILY FROM THE EFFECTS OF FOOT TRAFFIC WHICH ACCUMULATE NEAR THE CUP.

IN NEGOTIATING A 40-FOOT PUTT, YOU MAY WIND UP POKING THE BALL FAR PAST THE HOLE IF YOU BASE YOUR STROKE ON THE SPEED REQUIREMENTS OF THE MORE VISIBLE FIRST 20 FEET. CONSIDER A SPEED-UP FACTOR ON THE FINAL 20 FEET AND ALLOW FOR IT.